Spouses of Sex Addicts: Hope for the Journey

WORKBOOK

Spouses of Sex Addicts: Hope for the Journey

WORKBOOK

Françoise Mastroianni, LCPC, SEP, CADC, CCSAS,
Richard Blankenship, LPC, NCC, CCH, CCSAS

Alpharetta, Georgia

ISBN: 978-1-61005-335-8

Printed in the United States of America

♾This paper meets the requirements of ANSI/NISO Z39.48-1992 (Permanence of Paper)

Unless stated otherwise, all scripture passages were taken from: THE HOLY BIBLE, NEW INTERNATIONAL VERSION®, NIV® Copyright © 1973, 1978, 1984, 2011 by Biblica, Inc.™ Used by permission. All rights reserved worldwide.

Graphs from traumahealing.com are printed with permission from Peter A. Levine, PhD.

Checklist reprinted with permission of S-Anon International Family Groups, Inc., Nashville, TN. Compliance with S-Anon International Family Groups, Inc.'s copyrights and trademarks is required.

Test questions used with permission of The Office of Dr. Douglas Weiss, Heart to Heart Counseling Center. (719-278-3708).

Excerpt in Chapter 8 taken from *Boundaries* by Henry Cloud and John Townsend. Copyright © 1992 by (Copyright Holder). Use by permission of Zondervan. www.zondervan.com

The History and Philosophy of Your Emotions exercise from a training manual by The Gottman Institute. Copyright © 2000-2009 by Dr. John Gottman and Dr. Julie Schwartz Gottman. Distributed under license by The Gottman Institute, Inc.

This book is not intended to replace the need for therapy or counseling. Opinions in this book are provided for information purposes only and are not intended as a substitute for the therapeutic advice of a competent and knowledgeable counselor or psychologist/physiatrist. The reader should always consult a trusted counselor or doctor in matters relating to his/ her health and particularly with respect to any condition that may require immediate medical attention. The information provided in this book should not be construed as personal medical advice or instruction. Self-diagnosis and self-treatment is not recommended and may indeed be dangerous. Readers who fail to consult competent, trusted therapists assume the risk of any injuries or illness.
Names in the stories in *Spouses of Sex Addicts: Hope for the Journey (Workbook)* have been changed. Any resemblance to a specific person is coincidental. Steps have been taken to protect the identities of all individuals who contributed stories to this book.

Contents

Foreword

When the original book *S.A.R.A.H. (Spouses of Addicts Rebuilding and Healing)* was released in 2008, there were immediate requests for a workbook. It was being used in groups across the country and people wanted a resource for more practical application. Therapists wanted to be able to use it in therapy groups; support groups began reading and working through the material, churches and community organizations wanted to do more with the material.

In 2010, the updated version of the book was released under the title *Spouses of Sex Addicts: Hope for the Journey*. The new version included more resources and updated information. Once again, the requests for a workbook began to come in.

As a profession, the field of sexual addiction treatment is still relatively new (about thirty years old.) The treatment of spouses/partners of sex addicts is even newer and the information can become outdated very quickly. We are learning more about the impact of sexual addiction on spouses/partners and the implications for treatment.

Early pioneers in the field of sexual addiction treatment searched for ways to treat sexual addiction. Understandably, they looked to the 12-step model, which has helped drug addicts and alcoholics manage their addictions for decades. Sexual addiction has been partially managed through 12-step groups, though experts recognize that by itself, 12-step work is limited in its effectiveness. Organizations like L.I.F.E. Ministries International have taken the 12-steps and condensed them to 7 faith-based principles for Christians struggling with sexual addiction. Spouses and family members of alcoholics eventually developed Al-Anon, a 12-step program that would address the needs of spouses. Fellowships for sex addicts eventually developed S-Anon for the spouses/partners of sex addicts.

The assumption that the spouse can be treated as though they have their own "disease" has traumatized many who have sought help. Under the 12-step model, spouses/partners are assumed to be addicted to their addict and "sicker than their husbands." Labels such as "co-addict" and "codependent" are applied with frighteningly little thought and consideration of the impact upon the partner. This has led to what some now call "treatment induced trauma."

It does not matter that many partners knew nothing of the person's addiction prior to making a commitment. Nor does it matter that the partner may not have seen recognizable signs of the addiction's existence. The theory holds that partners develop co-addicted traits and characteristics over time due to the fact that they are in relationships with addicts.

In Barbara Steffens research, she found repeatedly that partners of sex addicts, described disclosure in word pictures filled with violent imagery, I knew they must be experiencing trauma and even Post Traumatic Stress Disorder (PTSD). I have heard women say that disclosure left them "shell shocked," "violated," "totally disoriented," "emotionally raped," and it was "like being stabbed repeatedly." Such destructive descriptions generally accompany traumatic events. Most startling was that 70 percent of the women met the symptomatic criteria for PTSD, in response to the disclosure of sexual addiction.[1]

In working with hundreds of spouses/partners of sex addicts through the years, we have seen people wounded beyond what words can describe. Many well-intentioned friends, family members, therapists, and churches inflict harm on spouses of sex addicts through harmful advice. The levels of trauma in partners of sex addicts are scary.

As a spouse, you are not to blame for the choices of the addict. You are profoundly impacted by them. We are wounded in relationships and we heal in relationships. The closer the relationship the more potential harm can be inflicted. At the same time, the closer the relationship, the more potential for life-giving intimacy exists.

Trauma keeps us from being present in the here and now. This workbook is meant to be a resource that will help integrate the physical, emotional, and spiritual dimensions of healing from the aftermath of trauma. Trauma is often stored in our bodies. Physical symptoms are one of the indicators of traumatic experience. Working with the physical aspects of trauma can help the body, heart, and mind heal. Sometimes called Somatic Experiencing (SE)[2], this is a process that is an organic self-regulating process that helps the body develop a large capacity to endure and release negative energy.

Discovery and disclosure of sexual infidelity in the relationship are a source of intense trauma. Trauma comes from the reality of the events and the meaning the

---

[1] Dr. Barbara Steffens, Speech on Spouses of Sex Addicts, October 2005, Cincinnati, Ohio.
[2] Somatic Experiencing (SE) is based on the work of Peter Levine and the Somatic Experiencing Trauma Institute. Levine is known for his book *"Waking the Tiger"* and his work in the field of trauma treatment.

victim assigns to the experiences. Long after the event has ceased, people will wrestle with the impact of the trauma in their lives.

Françoise Mastroianni came to me wanting to write a workbook for *Spouses of Sex Addicts: Hope for the Journey.* After watching Françoise work, hearing her story, and meeting her husband and members of her family, it was clear that she was the one who needed to write this book. Françoise knows the journey personally and professionally. She knows the pain of betrayal, the experience of trauma, and the power of a healing journey. As a clinician, she works with spouses/partners of sex addicts and couples in recovery from sexual addiction. She is a Certified Clinical Sexual Addiction Specialist (CCSAS) through the International Association of Certified Sexual Addiction Specialists. She is a Licensed Clinical Professional Counselor (LCPC), a Certified Alcohol and Drug Counselor (CADC). She is trained as a Level 11 EMDR specialist, and a Somatic Experiencing Practitioner (SEP). These are just a few of her credentials.

Your journey is sacred. The work you do, whether with a therapist, group, or on your own, is your story, your journey. This workbook is to be used as a doorway to your inner most thoughts and healing process. May God bless you in your discoveries and your experiences in the here and now. May you grow to know Him and trust Him with your pain and trauma wounds. May you experience safety, healing and empowerment, in body, mind, and spirit on the journey.

Richard Blankenship, LPC, NCC, CCH, CCSAS
www.cornerstoneprofessional.com

Chapter 1

I Can't Believe This Is Happening

With grief, the harder we try to avoid it, the heavier the burden becomes. The losses aren't clean. It's like someone came along and ripped part of your identity from your heart. (Spouses of Sex Addicts: Hope for the Journey – p. 28)

Finding out about my husband's addiction was one of the hardest moments in my life. A place I never expected to be after thirty-one years of marriage. I found out about his secret addiction to pornography while checking some airfares on line. Images of naked women and seductive poses popped up. He had forgotten to cover his tracks and did not delete the history. He got caught!

I was overwhelmed with grief, anger, embarrassment, pain, and humiliation. How could I have been married to my soul mate and best friend and not know that this had been an area of his life he kept from me for so many years. I was deeply wounded, and intuitively, I knew what I needed. I needed space and time alone to process the grief and violation against my mind, soul, spirit, and body. It was important to me that I could take the time I needed to get through the shock of the betrayal. I kept thinking, How could I not know this? and what flashed through my mind were the few incidences where this came up in the past and how he had denied and rationalized it. This time he was in the room with me and the images were right there on the screen, there was no hiding, no excuses and no one to blame.

Françoise

Grieving the Dreams that Were Lost

I want to start by acknowledging your willingness to engage in a workbook that can have positive results in the aftermath of discovering your spouse's sex addiction. I grieve with you. The emotional disconnect in the most important, valued primary adult relationship brings deep emotional pain.

The assignments in the workbook have been practiced by spouses in individual and group counseling. They are designed to develop an inner capacity to expand your awareness and functional range. Research and experience prove that when we are overwhelmed, our ability to be present and attuned to our needs and fears is limited. Our bodies go from being overwhelmed to shutting down. Over time, the fight, flight, or freeze takes us out of our functional range and inhibits our ability to ebb and flow in the stream of life's moments.

Any time you notice being overwhelmed and it feels like it may be beyond your ability to manage the exercises, take a moment to slow down and notice your breathing. Something as simple as noticing your breathing and feeling the experience of breathing in and throughout your body can be calming and help you to remember and understand what you're experiencing. Regardless of the pattern you have developed over time, you will need these skills and tools to take care of yourself.

My hope and prayer for you is that you experience a safe haven within your level of comfort as you build on your capacity to tune into your body, needs, and emotions.

Symptoms of Being Overwhelmed

The chart below is an example of what it may feel like when you are triggered and experience the symptoms of trauma. The symptoms can feel like un-discharged energy in your body, which can take you to the experience of feeling "overwhelmed or shut down."

Symptoms of Being Overwhelmed
(Above Line)

- High Anxiety
- Panic
- Hyperactivity
- Exaggerated Startle
- Inability to Relax
- Restlessness

- Hyper vigilance
- Digestive Problems
- Emotional Flooding
- Chronic Pain
- Sleeplessness
- Hostility/Rage

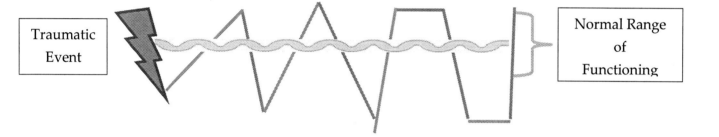

Traumatic Event

Normal Range of Functioning

Symptoms of Being Shut-Down
(Below Line)

- Depression
- Flat Affect
- Lethargy
- Deadness
- Exhaustion
- Chronic Fatigue

- Disorientation
- Disassociation
- Complex Syndromes
- Pain
- Low Blood Pressure
- Poor Digestion

www.traumahealing.com, used with permission of Peter A. Levine, PhD

Checking your subjective unit of distress periodically (SUDS) on a scale of 1–10 is a good check-in. By taking the time to do this, you slow yourself down and notice where you are with your thoughts, feelings, and anxiety level. If you are not overwhelmed by the exercise, you might want to continue working as long as you're feeling safe and in the "I can do this place." Limit your time with the assignments if your SUDS level is escalating. Be sure to take care of yourself throughout all the exercises in your workbook. Accessing difficult information can bring up difficult memories and be emotionally intense. There is more to you than your feelings. Slow down and breathe. Breathing in slow breaths will slow your body down. Be mindful of what else is going on with you; any thoughts, or meanings to what is happening, without self-judgment. It's a healthier way of working through the difficult stuff that comes up. It's tempting to completely avoid it, shut down, and not experience healing from the difficult memories and feelings.

As you practice this awareness, you will develop a greater capacity to experience the journey of healing, even through difficult emotions. Your feelings are important, yet they don't completely define you. Feeling out of control doesn't mean that you are a failure. It's the chaos inside and lack of organization around the issue that causes you to feel out of control. Trauma is chaotic. You will feel out of control at times. The chart below illustrates a more balanced system that helps you manage the internal chaos.

When my nervous system is balanced and my activation is low, I feel:

Open, curious	Relaxed yet alert
Embodied	Appropriatelly reactive
Available for connection	Able to be present
Fluid, resilient	Emotionally stable
Competent - a sense of mastery	Healthy - symptoms are manageable

I have choices and options

**I recognize when I am moving out of my functional range
and have tools to return to stability and stabilization
I know when to reach out for support
when I can't do it on my own**

www.traumahealing.com

You may also want to bring up a positive image as part of your self-care. Perhaps it's a place you have been or one you create in your mind's eye. Make this your "safe place," a visual that allows you to feel more grounded and stable in the midst of chaos. You can go to your "safe place" any time you need comfort. My image of a safe place is at the feet of Jesus. It gives me comfort and is a place I often seek to be. I have been there many times. My brain has an imprinted image of a loving Father, reaching out to me with tenderness and a caring heart.

You may be questioning whether or not you are a partner of a sex addict. Please take a moment with the following checklist. It may validate some of your own fears and confusion about sexual addiction and the devastating effects they have had on you. The following checklist is adapted from S-Anon, a Twelve-Step group for partners of sex addicts:

- Have you felt hurt or embarrassed by your spouse's sexual conduct?
- Have you secretly searched for clues about your spouse's sexual behavior?
- Have you lied about or covered up your spouse's sexual conduct?
- Have you had money problems because of your spouse's sexual behavior?
- Have you felt betrayed or abandoned by someone you loved and trusted?
- Are you afraid to upset your spouse for fear that he or she will leave you?
- Have you tried to control your spouse's sexual thoughts or behavior by doing things like throwing away pornography, dressing suggestively or being sexual with him or her in order to keep him or her from being sexual with others?
- Have you given into sex to try to keep peace in a relationship?
- Have you tried to convince yourself that your spouse's sexual thoughts and behavior shouldn't bother you?
- Have you doubted your attractiveness, your emotions and your sanity?
- Have you felt angry and/or stupid for not knowing about your spouse's acting out behavior?
- Have you engaged in uncomfortable, unwanted or physically dangerous sexual behavior?
- Has your preoccupation with your spouse's sexual thoughts and behavior affected your relationships with your children, your co-workers and/or other friends or family members?
- Have you neglected your physical and/or emotional health while in a relationship?

- Have you blamed other people, such as friends or sexual partners, society in general, his or her job, religion or birth family for your spouse's sexual behavior? Have you felt confused about what is true when talking with your spouse about his or her sexual thoughts or behavior? Have you avoided painful emotions by using drugs, alcohol or food or by being too busy?
- Do you find dealing with your spouse's sexual behavior or mood swings makes you feel crazy?
- Have you become a private investigator in your own home?
- Do you spend more time thinking about your spouse than you do yourself?
- Do you go through cycles of loving and then hating your spouse?
- Have you felt alone in your relationship or too ashamed to ask for help?[1]

    If you answer yes to any one of these questions, you may have been impacted one way or another—emotionally, psychologically, physically, or spiritually—by being in a relationship with a sex addict and you may benefit from these assignments.

Your life after discovery has been turned upside down. What you knew as a reality is now an illusion of what you thought was real. Your partner's sexual acting out has changed all of what seemed authentic and real to you. Start by writing what you know is real now; current circumstances, thoughts and feelings that are in the present as you experience life in the here and now.

---

[1] Reprinted with permission of S-Anon International Family Groups, Inc., Nashville, TN. Compliance with S-Anon International Family Groups, Inc.'s copyrights and trademarks is required.

Grief is a result of loss. Whether it's death, a health issue, a dream, or a betrayal, it is a painful process that is attached to many experiences. It comes in stages, never linear. Today you may find yourself angry at the addict and tomorrow you may be experiencing depression, shock and wondering how this could have ever happened to you. Denying or minimizing that this is a problem, bargaining with the addict to change or thinking, *How I will ever get through*? is all part of the grieving process. It is not unusual to think like this and have feelings that shift at random for someone who is experiencing what you are going through. Allow the grief the time it needs; you have every right to take that.

Grief as a deep sorrow and emotional wounding that causes us to experience mental distress as a result of our loss. Grief also has the ability to impact our emotional, physical and spiritual well being as a reaction to our loss. Grief and loss of this nature is dependent on the most important adult attachment you may have thought you had. Even though it is not a death of a loved one, it may feel like the death of a dream and life time together.

A bond was formed in your primary relationship as husband and wife and there is an internal injury, a loss that is experienced as a security attachment in the most important intimate relationship you have

"Attachment injuries" are related to the bond that was formed which Barbara Steffens refers to as "Relational Trauma:" "This occurs when one person betrays, abandons or refuses to provide support for another with whom he or she has developed an attachment bond."[2]

Wherever you are in the grieving process, take time to feel and experience the losses you have experienced. Know that you are not to blame for the addiction and the losses that have occurred as a result of the addict's acting-out behaviors. However, it is still painful, and brings up grief.

Take a pad of sticky notes, and for each loss you have experienced in the relationship with the addict, place the sticky note on the wall. This exercise will take time and you may want to do this with your therapist or as a group exercise. Allow yourself to notice and experience what comes up with each loss. Stay with your experience as much as you are able. As you become aware of your feelings, notice how much you can experience. What is manageable and tolerable? Slow down and be aware of what comes up for you. Do you have the ability to stay connected to your feelings, thoughts,

---

[2] Steffens, Barbara and Means, Marsha. *Your Sexually Addicted Spouse.* (Far Hills, NJ: New Horizon Press, 2009). Richard Blankenship, Barbara Steffens, and Marsha Means write extensively about relational trauma and the attachment wounds in sexually addictive relationships.

sensations, and behaviors, even if it was for a brief moment? Notice how it feels to write out the losses. Place them on a wall, and pay attention to any sensations in your body that you may experience. With trauma, it's easy to disregard these sensations and feelings, and focus on the cognitive thoughts that keep you in your head, and not the integrated whole self.

The "felt sense" is a sensation in your body and not the same as a feeling. It's experienced as a physical sensation such as a pounding in your heart or twitching in your gut when you are feeling sad or upset about something. I want to take all precautions as I assign these exercises, mainly because you are likely to be alone doing the assignments. My hope is that as we move along you will have a growing capacity to tolerate the activation that comes up and the tools to deactivate the negative energy. Most of the exercises are experiential and meant to be shared in a safe group setting. There is healing in numbers. Thoughts, feelings, and stories are validated as we share our most vulnerable self. If you are not able to get through this on your own, call on a safe person for help. If you are in a group, get each other's names and e-mail addresses and support one another wherever you are in the process.

Use this workbook as a journal to be authentic with your feelings and thoughts. Find a place where you can be comfortable and feel safe to journal your experiences. Take a moment to check in with yourself.

1. What was most noticeable for you in the sticky note exercise?

Take the time to notice where in your body you feel the grief. See if you can be aware of where that is; shoulders, stomach, chest or any other area and notice what the sensation may be. Stay with it long enough to be curious about it. The sensation might be achy, tight, tense, trembling, fluttery, pounding, throbbing, or clenched. It's your body's expression of your feelings.

Bringing yourself into the here and now will heighten your present awareness and maintain the ability to stay in your functional range. Try wiggling your toes, rotating your wrist, tapping or rubbing your arms and legs. Becoming more aware of your own system enlarges your tolerance level to engage in these difficult assignments. Track yourself for any shift or settling, no matter how small or large.

2. What changed, what dissipated, what became quieter, larger, brighter, or softer?

3. Where do you think you are presently in the Grief Cycle Model?

Five Stages of Grief - Elisabeth Kübler Ross	
	Interpretation
1 **Denial**	Denial is a conscious or unconscious refusal to accept facts, information, reality, etc., relating to the situation concerned. It's a defense mechanism and perfectly natural. Some people can become locked in this stage when dealing with a traumatic change that can be ignored. Death of course is not particularly easy to avoid or evade indefinitely.
2 **Anger**	Anger can manifest in different ways. People dealing with emotional upset can be angry with themselves and/or with others, especially those close to them. Knowing this helps others keep detached and non-judgmental when experiencing the anger of someone who is very upset.
3 **Bargaining**	Traditionally the bargaining stage for people facing death can involve attempting to bargain with whatever God the person believes in. People facing less serious trauma can bargain or seek to negotiate a compromise. For example "Can we still be friends?" when facing a break-up. Bargaining rarely provides a sustainable solution, especially if it's a matter of life or death.
4 **Depression**	Also referred to as preparatory grieving. In a way it's the dress rehearsal or the practice run for the 'aftermath' although this stage means different things depending on whom it involves. It's a sort of acceptance with emotional attachment. It's natural to feel sadness and regret, fear, uncertainty, etc. It shows that the person has at least begun to accept the reality.
5 **Acceptance**	Again this stage definitely varies according to the person's situation, although broadly it is an indication that there is some emotional detachment and objectivity. People dying can enter this stage a long time before the people they leave behind, who must necessarily pass through their own individual stages of dealing with the grief.

Based on the Grief Cycle model first published in *On Death & Dying*, Elisabeth Kübler-Ross, (New York: Schribner,1969). Interpretation by Alan Chapman 2006-2009.[3]

---

[3] http://www.businessballs.com/elisabeth_kubler_ross_five_stages_of_grief.htm

Our bodies hold the memory of the trauma. It may be experienced in the pit of your stomach, pressure on your chest, or tension in your neck or back. After discovery/disclosure, your entire being may experience any one of these responses for survival at any given time. People who survive serious auto accidents may go into freeze, when triggered as a threat response for survival, and report not remembering the collision. This is the body's way of surviving horrific trauma. Over time, many traumatic events can accumulate and feel overwhelming.

When there has been a violation, a threat to the body, mind, and spirit and in the event of sexual addiction, experiencing the loss of the relational trauma, our bodies go into protective mode to defend us. Trauma can stay frozen within us for long periods of time. This can lead to symptoms such as: hyper-arousal, constriction, dissociation, freezing, hyper-vigilance, flashbacks, hyperactivity, exaggerated emotional or startle responses, nightmares, mood swings and reduced ability to deal with stress, depression, feelings of detachment, alienation and isolation.[4]

---

[4] www.traumahealing.com

4. Recall a time in your grieving experience when you were in a highly emotional state and unable to manage the attempts to control and stabilize the effects of the trauma. It may have been early on when you first heard of or discovered the addiction, or perhaps something that triggered your grief later on in your healing process. Journal about that time in the space below.

Event:
What is happening in your body now? Notice any awareness of trauma energy, in the event that it may be trapped. Breathe!
How is it at this moment in time, to sit with the memory and what you are experiencing?
As you remembered the experience, can you recall the moment back then, when you knew you would be alright?
Knowing that you had resources then, and you were able to get through, can you be alright for now?

What was your strength?

Our brain is an incredibly complex organ. The limbic system involves our emotions and particularly those involved in the threat response, fight, flight, and freeze. These emotions include fear, anger, and feelings related to sexual behaviors. The amygdala is part of this system and processes negative emotions as well as the pleasurable ones. It is also responsible for memories that are stored. It is known as part of the brain that stores emotional memory. In short, the amygdala picks up the danger warnings, , the limbic system, particularly the amygdala is like a pilot and its counterpart the hypothalamus is the co-pilot. Once the copilot receives instruction from the pilot, it instructs the pituitary and adrenal glands to release the stress hormones and do a take-off into the blood stream.

Your response to a threatening situation and particularly to your spouse's sexual addiction may be to go into fight, perhaps your response is flight, a form of avoidance. Or, you may freeze and feel emotionally paralyzed and disengage from the hard painful reality. Become familiar with the pattern and emotions that you experience to manage the pain. When the switch board is communicating with headquarters, the frontal cortex, it makes for a safer landing. The headquarters is not fully engaged when the limbic system is on the alert. The pilot, the amygdala, becomes the chief in command. The ride is much smoother when all systems are in check.

Wherever you are in the healing process, you deserve the space and time it takes to heal. An honest search for stability and relief from suffering can be the driving force that keeps us moving out of the "stuck on/off" place. When emotions come up around any memories or triggers, notice the body sensations and feelings. It's your body's way of getting your attention and needing some time to slow down. Your ability to think clearly may not be totally accessible. The control feels good and needed at the time. However, as you get stronger and more confident in your ability to manage your internal experiences, control becomes less of a need. Think of it as going through three phases: phase one equals lots of control; phase two equals stabilization; phase three equals letting go of control. The letting-go process does not mean, "he is off the hook," what he's done never means that it will ever be forgotten. The "F" word, forgiveness, is part of the healing process, it takes time to get there, and before you're ready to forgive you will vacillate between the three phases, until you're ready to decide where you want to land.

5. What threat response are you most likely to experience in the event of a trigger? Fight, Flight or Freeze?

Are you aware of what is going on in that moment?
Then what happens?

Being in the present is being in the here and now. Orienting yourself to your environment and what you notice by bringing your senses into it. What do you hear, smell and what are you observing? Our bodies are not made to be in the threat response for long periods of time. We suffer physically, emotionally and psycho-logically when enduring intense trauma. How have I gotten through my grief so far?

What are my coping skills :

If your coping skills are no longer working for you, is there one thing you can do different right now?

What helps you stay in the present?

Notice where in your body you sense stability; your feet, back, hands, shoulders or perhaps your core. Stay with this long enough to experience what the feeling is and what the sensation is like for you. Scan your body from head to toe and notice where there is a sense of stability and connection in your body.

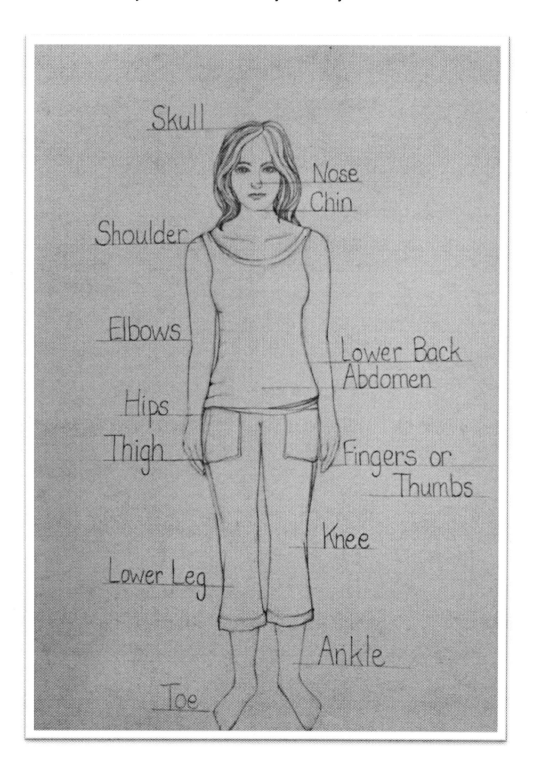

Stabilization can be experienced as: Calm, Energized, Smooth, Streaming, Warm, Cool, Relaxed, Open, Light, Spacious, Airy, Releasing, Expanded, Bubbly, Expansive, Flowing, Tingling, Floating, Fluid, Discharging, and Grounded. Scan your body from head to toe and notice where you experience a strong sense of self.

When I notice my... I feel... The felt sense is...

When I notice my... I feel... The felt sense is...

When I notice my... I feel... The felt sense is...

When I notice my... I feel... The felt sense is...

6. Circle any sensations you have ever experienced.

Achy	Dark	Knotted	Sore
Blocked	Dense	Nauseous	Spacey
Breathless	Disconnected	Nervy	Suffocated
Bruised	Dizzy	Numb	Tender
Bumpy	Dull	Pounding	Tickly
Bubbly	Electric	Prickly	Tense
Burning	Energetic	Queasy	Thick
Buzzy	Fluttery	Radiating	Throbbing
Clenched	Frozen	Referring	Tight
Closed	Heavy	Relaxed	Tingling
Cold	Hollow	Sensitive	Trembling
Congested	Icy	Shaky	Twitchy
Constricted	Itchy	Shivery	Wobbly
Contracted	Jagged	Smooth	Wooden

7. List the sensations you circled and what you remember about them.

1.	
2.	
3.	
4.	
5.	
6.	
7.	
8.	
9.	
10.	

In *Spouses of Sex Addicts: Hope for the Journey*, Melissa Haas wrote, *"I felt so out of control. One minute I would be fine and the next minute tears would be running down my face. I wasn't going crazy, though, I was simply grieving."* (SOSA, p. 33)

8. Does Melissa's experience resonate with you and if so, how?

Telling your story is an important part of your healing journey. Integrating the experience by writing it and telling it is validating and affirming.

Before you start this assignment take a moment to orient yourself to your environment. Be in your space and be safe with it. Is it a particular room, do you need your shoes off, a special chair, music or quiet? Scan the room for anything that may interrupt the flow of your journaling. Notice the space for range of mobility, just in case you need to stretch your arms or move your legs. Pay attention to what happens in your core in the moments that are especially difficult. Check in with your SUDS level and take care of yourself. Slow down if you need to. You are about to write your story, your thoughts, feelings and whatever else you choose to add to it. If you are going to read your story in group, I would recommend one story per evening, giving yourself and group members time to process and validate your experience regarding the betrayal and the relational trauma. I recommended that you do this with the help of a trained facilitator.

Take your time and write your story. There is healing in writing and sharing it with safe people. Knowing that there are others in similar situations that understand your pain can give meaning to what you are going through.

9. Take the next few pages or more if you need it to write "your story."

What was it like writing your story? What do you need for yourself right now?

Hope for the Heart

"…I will never leave you nor forsake you." Joshua 1:5

My challenge for today is:

Leah's Story

I had no proof; no evidence; nothing but a strong sense that wouldn't allow me to be convinced otherwise this time. There was absolutely nothing he could say or do which would make me believe he wasn't lying. He wasn't going to make me feel guilty or "drop it" like all the other times I had asked in the past. There was a powerful voice inside. A very calm, clear, and loud voice that I couldn't ignore. My intuition was guiding me, and I knew I couldn't choose anything other than confronting my husband that day. I was scared to death, but strangely confident that I already knew the truth and fueled by my anger, I was determined to hear it from his mouth. I didn't want to be right. I was praying to be wrong because I knew what I didn't want my reality to be. My heart pounded out of my chest as I gave him my ultimatum. "Either you come clean now…you're an addict and need help and then maybe we will have a chance to make it. Or I will find out on my own…it's only a matter of time until I do and when I do, I'm filing for divorce.

My heart dropped into the pit of my stomach when I saw his face. Time slowed down. My body forgot how to breathe. I felt an intense surge of adrenaline and when they say fight, flight or freeze…let me tell you I wanted to fight! I had never felt anything like it before. My core was on fire like a volcano about to erupt. My hands wanted to beat him and throw whatever was in reach. But, I couldn't. I had to just sit there and feel this extreme energy pump through me and resist the urgency to do the things my body wanted me to do. Even though everything in my being told me I was right two days before the confrontation, it wasn't until my husband began his confession that the shock crept in. My brain felt like it was submerged in a thick gel. I felt so confused. I had a hard time just listening and couldn't talk. As I heard him admit that he had been using pornography, the only thought recycling over and over in my head was, "I can't believe this is happening!" My head repeatedly shook back and forth in disbelief. I couldn't believe that my husband had been lying to me for over two years…that he actually looked me in my eyes and lied right to my soul.

Who could he be if he was capable of such deceit and betrayal? What kind of person did I choose to spend the rest of my life with? Who was he really? What part of our relationship was real? I couldn't stop all these questions from bombarding me. I just couldn't believe this was the truth. What does this mean about him, me, and us? What will happen to my life as it began to crumble apart? I could not comprehend what was happening and the magnitude of the consequences it was about to bring to my life. In the days and months following the truth about my husband's addiction and what behaviors he had engaged in throughout our relationship, that feeling of complete and utter disbelief remained and spiked each and every time I would hear new information. Will this ever end? Even over a year later and with my husband in recovery, I am still constantly reminded of my reality. A reality that I never could have imagined or wanted for myself and for my son. A reality that I would not have chosen. A reality that will always be here as long as I remain in my marriage.

Today, when I am triggered, I still can't believe that this is happening; that my husband is a sex addict and has to work so hard to not bring more damage and devastation into our lives. The fear and myriad emotions that took over me, and still can, will forever be inside me. They are less intense now and most of the time manageable because I am stronger now than I have ever been. But this experience has permanently changed me and my life...without my permission. Fortunately, through the darkness, we have both grown and it has been the catalyst to helping us become who we've always hoped to be. I can only pray that we both continue to travel down this path and on this journey our Higher Power has planned for us.

Leah

My Journal

My thoughts for today:

My feelings:

What am I sensing in my body?

Can I put any meaning to my experiences?

What can I be thankful for today?

Chapter Two

Trauma and Betrayal

As the spouse of a sex addict, you are a trauma survivor. Your wounds must be treated with the best care available. (SOSA P. 46)

As I sat in disbelief and cried till I could no longer feel the pain. My body felt numb, and my mind was not able to grasp my new reality. I had moments of disparity that led me to believe that I was not good enough and never would be. How could I compare to the brushed and polished images that he examined and lusted after? I felt used and objectified. My heart and spirit felt the sadness of the betrayal and my body felt like it wanted to collapse in disbelief. I lost my sense of confidence in who I was as a woman and wife. The energy was drained right out of my body. I experienced deep sadness and no motivation to take care of myself and my basic needs. I had memories of moments we had together that now seemed futile; that had no meaning. I questioned our relationship and wondered if I ever was the special one, and did these images of other women come up in the presence of our intimacy. How often did he view pornography and how long had he been doing this? My mind was relentless. It felt like an invasion in my body that went through every muscle, nerve and bone that I had. I wanted to turn the clock back; I did not want this to be my new reality. But this, I knew, was to forever change me, change us. I could not look back, nor change the past. This was not anything I signed up for.

I looked to the one I knew would bring be through this, in His ever so gentle way, I heard His voice in my mind saying, I am here with you, trust Me, I will not leave you or forsake you. We have an awesome God and I am thankful for the way He carried me through some of my darkest moments.

Françoise

Judy

My brain could not function; it could not absorb what was happening; I couldn't filter what was relevant and what was not; I could not process the situation and what it meant to my past and future. Simple tasks were overwhelming while my brain raced to process all the changes it was being asked to accept.

My heart raced whenever the thought of my situation crossed my brain. I paced the house for hours with my heart pounding. I did not have a literal heart attack but my heart was broken in a way far deeper than the way that phrase is often tossed around.

Judy's range of functioning was compromised and impeded by internal threats that she had no control of. Trauma disorients your heart, mind, and body. Attunement and connection to the deeper self is fragmented and lost with trauma. Judy experienced mental blankness, hyper-arousal, reduced ability to deal with the problem, impending doom, dissociation, constriction, freezing and much more.

1. What were your symptoms like at the onset of the initial trauma?

| |
| |
| |
| |
| |
| |
| |
| |

My body may not have been dying like a person in medical shock but my being was. I was entering recovery from an emergency that changed my life and who I am. I needed calming, and support. I needed the care given to a patient who is suffering a great trauma. I needed meals. I needed help remembering things. I needed security. I needed a way to escape the trauma long enough to get real sleep. I needed help identifying a person in my life I could share this with and depend on for help. I needed to talk and to say things over and over until they began to feel real. I needed security and safety. I needed intensive care—I was in shock.

2. What were your needs then and what are they now?

| |
| |
| |
| |
| |
| |
| |

3. Describe what your best "functional range" is, i.e., able to stay present with your experience, self, and available to connect with others. How do you know when you're out of your functional range? What is that like for you?

| |
| |
| |
| |
| |
| |
| |

Stabilization and moving through the trauma is a process of learning to self-regulate, expand self-awareness, the capacity to let go of the negative energy, and an effective means of dealing with the trauma. A system that ebbs and flows, activates and deactivates the residual negative energy, is a system that is moving in and out of the three phases "out of control, stabilization, and letting go" in a functional range. Recognize when you are approaching too much stimulation and be aware of what you need to do to return to a safe place. As you move through the healing process, you will have a greater sense of trusting your ability to restore safety and stability when triggers come up.

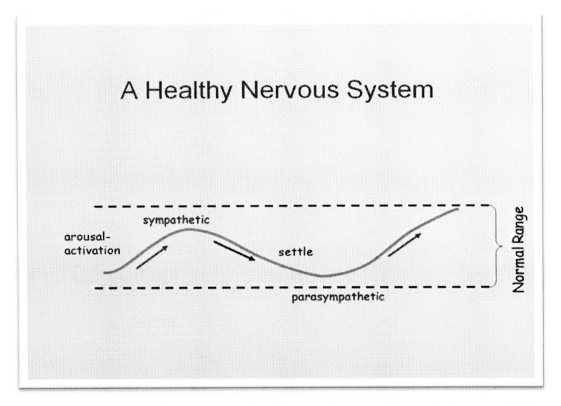

www.traumahealing.com, used with permission of Peter A. Levine, PhD

A system that is in a healthy functional range ebbs and flows with activation and deactivation.

"The pain of betrayal becomes impossible to capture in words. What do you say when the person you have trusted with your heart has deceived, betrayed and psychologically tortured you?" (SOSA, p. 46)

Rhonda

I don't know how I can recover from this. The level of betrayal and the cruelty of your mind games defy anything I've seen in all of my years on this earth. You love inflicting pain and humiliation. I misjudged you completely. You have no conscience. I gave you the very best I had. We were a great team. It could have been greater. The worst part is I still love you. And I am so loyal that I want to restore our relationship. I miss your touch and the comfort and safety it brought with it. You fooled me- it was only an illusion.

The betrayal in the relationship that Rhonda is alluding to was her deepest attachment bond, and as the primary adult attachment bond it has potential to hurt and heal at the very core of your heart. What she had grown to believe and to know as her reality was shattered. Her greatest fear left her in shock, and her expression of the brokenness had "severely harmed her trust in people."

4. Write a letter to your spouse or ex about your experience after discovery/ disclosure, and how the betrayal may still be hurting and bringing up the symptoms of trauma, such as nightmares, and inability to trust anyone. At the end of the letter, write down what you are doing about it. "I am doing the best I can, I am in therapy, I am making new friends that support me, I am much more aware of whom I am and what I want and what I will not allow."

This does not mean he has to see your letter. You may experience this exercise as de-activating; it may be just what you need to release some of the charge that is in your system around this issue.

Upon Discovery:

Rhonda struggled with her faith in God as a result of the trauma/betrayal: *I now doubt God and can't even connect with Him. My faith is destroyed.*

Is this something you can relate to? Rhonda states later on in her story that "it was worth the pain, and in spite of this, there is hope for the journey." You may or may not be at that place, or choose to go there. What is real for you now is your present reality and how you experience it.

God knows your pain. "I have chosen you and not rejected you. Do not fear, for I am with you. Do not anxiously look about you, for I am your God. I will strengthen you, surely I will help you. Surely I will uphold you with my righteous right hand" (Isaiah 41:10). God used this in Rhonda's life as something she could be thankful for in the end. She also wanted her story to be told and used as a means of inspiring hope where there seems to be so little with sex addiction. It's not over for Rhonda, there are days when her emotional rollercoaster is out of control, and she needs help to manage the intense feelings she experiences.

Developing safety and stability is essential for your healing process. Getting to know your range of functionality and expanding your experience in a healthy range of ebbing and flowing.

The process is long and arduous, and yet, we do have a greater source outside of ourselves to help us through the journey. God is greater than any other!

5. Where is God in your life now? How is He making Himself real to you? I met with a friend whose spiritual beliefs are different than mine; however, in a moment of deep sadness she cried out to God for help, and within an hour she received a call from her friend that was compelled to offer her professional services without charging her—something she could not afford—and yet needed for some mental clarity. My friend saw this as a "God moment." Wherever you are in your spiritual journey, God is saying, "I am your God, surely I will help you." Surely He desires the very best for us.

| **Dear God:** |
| |
| |
| |
| |
| |
| |
| |
| |

"The final chapter in your life and relationship isn't finished. Your story is still being written…" (SOSA, p. 46)

6. Rhonda states: "it was worth the pain, and there is hope for the journey!" Where do you think she is coming from, and can you connect her experience with your reality?

| |
| |
| |
| |
| |
| |
| |

Hope for the Heart

"Stand at the crossroads and look; ask for the ancient paths, ask where the good way is, and walk in it, and you will find rest for your souls." Jeremiah 6:16a

My challenge for today is:

Sally's Story

I have experienced many betrayals due to my husband's sex addiction. Each time my body responded physically and with increased intensity. The first discovery that something was not quite right in my marriage was when I found a condom wrapper while cleaning out the car. My heart raced, my body began to shake and my legs gave out from underneath me. The moments following that discovery I was in a dreamlike state; I felt as though I was no longer connected to my body. My whole world came crashing down around me and I didn't recognize what was left. Each time that I thought my husband was in recovery and I discovered a new betrayal, my symptoms worsened and it took longer for me to recover.

The next discovery was that my husband was not in recovery from his sex addiction. He told me that he was no longer in recovery and left for treatment out of state. I didn't know what he had done; just that he had done something. Up until that point, I thought he was in recovery. Again, I felt as if I was in a dream world, only it was a nightmare. It was as if the world was continuing and I was standing still. I spent that day unable to get out of bed, switching between sobbing and just feeling numb. I lost what had been my reality and was thrown into a new world once again. My husband had broken our marriage vows again; he had lied. We were living a lie and now I was left to pick up the pieces and take care of our four-year-old son. The pain of living in my new reality was too much.

I began to disconnect from the world. I withdrew from my friends and family. I didn't know who to trust or talk to. I so badly wanted my old world back. I wanted to feel safe in my home; to be able to enjoy being with others. Looking back on this time period, I don't know how I made it through; how I continued to do the day-to-day tasks at home and work. There were times that I was so disconnected from the world that I would forget to eat, forget to feed my son. Only when he looked at me and said, "Mommy, I'm hungry; when are we going to eat?" would I realize that it was well past dinnertime. I would walk around the house, the grocery store, work unable to focus on anything. My eyes were constantly scanning, moving around, and unsure of what I was even looking for. At times I couldn't remember what I had just done or I would forget what I was doing in the middle of a simple task.

As the months passed while my husband was in treatment, I struggled with day-to-day life. I managed to do it but was so disconnected from it all. Many times I felt like the walking dead; there but not really there. I couldn't believe this was my life! What had I done to deserve this? At first I disassociated from my world at home in order to function; to continue working and taking care of my son. Eventually it got to the point that I would be playing with my son and find myself disassociating from the world. I would come back into the room to my son saying my name over and over to get my attention.

One of the many difficult things that happened was that I became extremely uncomfortable with physical touch from anyone, at times even from our son. I began to experience an intense anxiety in my daily life. It would hit me when I was working, when I saw the word massage, or a pretty woman. Something as simple as a friend asking me how I was would send me into a panic. I couldn't really be honest and yet I felt discontent with lying. Eventually I avoided the question altogether by avoiding people. I didn't answer the phone, and didn't leave my office at work. Sometimes the anxiety would hit me completely out of nowhere.

I began to have difficulty sleeping. I had nightmares and would lay paralyzed in my bed when I woke up in the middle of the night. The normal creaking of our house sent me into a panic so intense that I was paralyzed. With the repeated betrayals I found myself barely keeping my head above water. I carried a notebook with me at work so that I could write down things that I needed to do. If I didn't do this I would forget by the time I left a meeting what I was supposed to do. Prior to this all happening, I had an excellent memory. My mind was so focused on protecting myself from feeling the pain again that I didn't have room for anything more.

Sally

My Journal

My thoughts for today:

My feelings:

What am I sensing in my body?

Can I put any meaning to my experiences?

What can I be thankful for today?

Chapter Three

Wounded: Heart, Soul, Mind and Spirit

Because of the way you have learned to manage trauma, it will impact the way you cope with your new trauma. (SOSA, P. 47)

What was familiar to me, no longer had the same compelling attraction to manage my everyday affairs. It was difficult to function and all I could do was. to sit in my disparity and disbelief. I couldn't eat, sleep or be around anyone for days. I requested that my husband tell our adult children, I didn't want any more secrets, and did not want to be responsible for any of his stuff. He had created this mess and I needed him to take ownership. One evening, late into the night, my husband appeared at the door. I let him in, since I had asked him to leave, and he fell at my feet weeping and asking for my forgiveness. We both fell to the floor and cried in each other's arms for the pain that his addiction brought into our relationship. The deceit and lies had wounded my heart, mind, soul, and us, our relationship. I could no longer trust him; whatwas true and what was a lie? I was sixteen when I met him, my first love, he had shattered my hopes and dreams for the future. And at that time it seemed like I would not get beyond the next moment.

My mind could not make sense of this; why would he risk losing his family . How could he keep a secret from me for all these years? My soul was deeply grieved by the lies and dismissal of me. My spirit cried out to God: I need your strength, courage and healing to get through this. I don't know if I can do this Lord. Do I have the capacity to move forward? Will I ever be able to take him back into my heart and learn to trust him again?.

Françoise

Trauma may be a single horrific event; it can also be a series of smaller events that impact your life over a period of time. Trauma has a cumulative effect. The experience of discovering your spouse's sexual addiction is an assault to your mind, body, spirituality, and so many other aspects of the relationship. Dr. Barbara Steffens researched partners' of sex addicts and discovered that 70% of spouses, upon disclosure, developed symptoms of post-traumatic stress disorder (PTSD). Listed below are a few of the symptoms reported by women that have experienced trauma and violation in the relationship.

- It left me shell shocked
- I threw up, couldn't sleep, couldn't eat and cried constantly
- I felt horror, anger, rage, terror, fury at God
- I frequently had disturbing dreams and nightmares
- My initial reaction was to shake uncontrollably; I've had this reaction before to someone's death. It was a death.[5]

In Rhonda's story she reports; "I'm fighting to concentrate. I caught myself zoning out a lot today. It was hard to stay focused. I had another nightmare about you; I've been plagued with these nightmares for over a year. I wonder if they will ever stop." (SOSA P. 44)

"One of the first things you need to ask is, how did you survive this? This is amazing that you are still here. It's amazing that you still have the guts to go on with your life. What is allowing you to function? What are you good at? What gives you comfort?" (SOSA, p.48)

Take a moment to slow yourself down, check in with your breathing, orient to the present, and notice where in your body your feel strong. Also, notice your environment and your sense of safety. Be aware of colors, textures, smells and sounds. This can help you feel grounded and stronger while managing the hard stuff.

---

[5] Steffens and Means. *Your Sexually Addicted Spouse.* p. 18.

1. How do you manage to stay in your safe place when things outside of your control seem to be escalating?

2. What gives you purpose, strength, and allows you to function?

3. What are your strengths?

4. What gives you and has given you comfort, peace, and reason to move forward?

| |
| |
| |
| |
| |
| |

Leah's trauma symptoms were off the chart after finding out what she intuitively knew about her husband's secret life with a woman she trusted with her children and had known for many years. Her heart was deeply broken.

"Please send out prayers for me. I am not doing well at all. My husband just revealed that he has been in love with the babysitter since last summer and that they have been sleeping together in my home and then in his mother's home since last fall. I am numb and devastated. I can't stop crying and sleep eludes me. He claims that she broke up with him and that they are not seeing each other, but I don't believe that to be true. When will the heartbreak end? When will the tornado end? Any advice to get through this pain is welcome. I am hurting deep."

This picture exemplifies what the "tornado" feels like for Leah. The information or event that is triggered is overwhelming. The trauma takes us deep into despair. As Leah expresses *"crying and sleep eludes me."* It feels like a "tornado."

Rate the level of distress you've ever experienced with each symptom.
(SUDS) of 1-10 (10 being the highest level of distress.)

Trauma Symptom	What was going on around the time that you experienced the symptom of distress ?	1–10
Sleep difficulties		
Headaches		
Weight loss		
Anxiety attacks		
Nightmares		
Flashbacks		
Spacing, numbing		
Outbursts of anger		
Uncontrollable crying		
Memory problems		
Suicidal thoughts		
Passing out		
Feeling tense		
Recurring images, thoughts, feelings		
Hyper vigilance		
Lack of trust		
Lack of concentration		
Restricted range of emotions		
Lack of interest		
Isolation		
Feeling detached		
Sense of doom		

5. Circle any item listed in the above table that has a 5-6 or higher distress level, write the trauma symptom in the table below. Indicate how you have managed this symptom in the past, how you are coping with it today, and how you would like to manage it in the future.

Trauma Symptom	Past	Present	Future

6. Trauma is addressed in four categories. "Physical, emotional, sexual, and spiritual trauma and can take many forms. These are usually direct and invasive, and clearly impact people in negative ways." (SOSA, p.50-57).

- Physical Abuse will take the form of assault upon a person's body. Hitting, slapping, pushing, shoving, and other forms of intimidation involving bodily contact, inflict physical trauma on one's personhood.
- Emotional abuse can take the form of yelling, screaming, name calling, and any other form of verbal abuse.
- Sexual abuse covers behaviors, such as touching or penetrating the genital area, teasing about the body, inaccurate information about sexuality.
- Spiritual abuse can take the form of messages about an angry and punitive God.

Wounds of Abandonment and Neglect:

- Physical neglect can involve being left alone without proper supervision. It could be there was not adequate food, clothing, or shelter.
- Emotional abandonment may be that you were not heard as a child. Perhaps no nurturing or caring was directly expressed.
- Sexual neglect takes place when there is a failure to provide proper sex education.
- Spiritual neglect here may have been a failure to model spiritual disciplines or a failure to present a picture of God that includes love, acceptance, and grace, which will impair spiritual development.

7. Write down the wounds you have experienced in each of these four categories. (Reference book pages 50–57 for more information on these types of traumas.) Include both invasive traumas and wounds of neglect/abandonment.

Invasive Traumas, Physical
Wounds of Neglect/Abandonment, Physical
Invasive Traumas, Emotional
Wounds of Neglect/Abandonment, Emotional

Wounds of Neglect/Abandonment, Emotional
Invasive Traumas, Sexual
Wounds of Neglect/Abandonment, Sexual
Invasive Traumas, Spiritual
Wounds of Neglect/Abandonment, Spiritual

8. What are you noticing and experiencing now, after this exercise?

Managing Emotional Needs:

When experiencing trauma, managing your emotional needs can sometimes make you feel like you are in the pit of despair. The trauma takes on a life of its own, and seems to dominate your every thought, action and experience. The moments seem to disappear, and it's difficult to stay in the here and now, because it all seems so overwhelming. The children's needs may get neglected, your needs are at the bottom of the list, things don't get done as you would like them to, and your spouse may not be around to support and help out. The cycle continues to perpetuate the trauma.

When there is a threat to your emotional safety and security you will naturally be overwhelmed with fear and anxiety. Slow yourself down and become aware of your breathing. Your brain and body will be better equipped to assess and manage the threat. Take a deep, slow breath, and a nice slow exhale. This creates a calming effect by slowing down the cardiovascular and respiratory systems. Notice what the feeling may be that comes up and stay with it as long as you can. Lean into it long enough to break the pattern that keeps you stuck and detached. Notice what it is like to be with the feelings that come up and see if you can be curious about what it might be like to move away from it or towards it in incremental stages.

For some, anger is a scary place to be, because last time they were angry they lost control, and were not aware of anything but their anger. They get "stuck on." There is no stopping when the roller coaster starts up. It's like being suspended in mid-air, and the fear up there is that they're never going to come back down. The crash from the descent plunges them into the shame pit, failure, and depression. A pattern for most that is painful and has caused many losses as well as physical pain.

Beth

Beth suffers the disparity and agony of anger outburst, beating herself up emotionally with shame and fear. *"It's my fault, what's wrong with me, I am not normal, other people don't react like this."* Beth grew up in a family where yelling/screaming and physically abusing each other was how they related. Beth and I are working towards befriending her anger, not being afraid of it. Noticing when it's there and leaning into it long enough to acknowledge its presence without being engulfed and swallowed by it.

Being in an abusive family, Beth learned early on how to take care of herself. When she screamed at the top of her lungs, she got the attention she wanted, just not in the way it was meant to be. And so the pattern developed into a style that was familiar to her based on her relationships with her primary caregivers. Her fight response to threatening situations is what got her through adolescence and some difficult times as her family went through a divorce. This became the pattern of coping, amongst the drugs and suicidal attempt.

The intense activation, with no discharge/release, kept her feeling out of control. After many years of this level of activation, Beth suffered with physical problems, and partly the result of the inflammation caused from the amount of cortisol pumping through her body in the constant state of hyper arousal. She now, after years of therapy, has the capacity and tools to stay in her functional range and presence of mind to be in the here and now when her nervous system is activated.

It is normal to attempt to protect ourselves, however, without the discharge and holding unto the incomplete response it can be displaced, and in Beth's case, it led to self-destructive behaviors. When pornography showed up in her marriage, her reactions were not any different to what had been familiar as a child. Beth wanted to learn how to control her responses appropriately and be present with what she was experiencing. She wanted to have the capacity to increase her internal awareness and ability to manage the threat in her system. Beth has become aware of her body sensations and notices the irritations and frustrations as she feels the ride coming on. She is able to take a time out to self-care, breathe, and journal her thoughts as she slows the process down. It's a healthy way to deactivate some of the negative energy.

Remember that the process of healing is never linear. One moment you will be enraged at the addict's behavior or lack of it, and another completely shut down. In this next exercise imagine in your mind's eye a container that is a holding place for what you have no control of. The stuff that we sometimes try to manage may not be ours and provides an unhealthy distraction.

My Container:

Things I cannot control.

Draw a picture of your container, a place where you can put people, places, thoughts and memories that distract you from being present.

9. Write a letter to yourself, as though you were receiving it from a friend who cares about you and your feelings. Be sure to be gentle with your words. At the end of this exercise comment on what it was like to experience love and kindness towards yourself.

My dearest self:

Managing your physical needs:

"Worn out" may be the words that resonate at this stage of your journey since the discovery of your spouse's sexual addiction. It is as important to take the time to slow yourself down physically, as it is emotionally, and be kind to yourself. The tendency may be to stay busy, and do more, because, of course, it hurts to stay with the emotional pain. The kind of time I am referring to is an intentional "take-care-of- my-body" need.

Exercise stimulates the neurotransmitter serotonin and you can actually feel better. It also allows for more balance and calm in your life. You may be in the wake of the bare threads of this neurotransmitter, because of the constant stress that's been there for weeks, months, and for some, years. You might want to make an appointment with a psychiatrist. There are medications that can be helpful. Be practical and realistic when it comes to exercise. For example, if you have never run in your life, it does not make sense to start running, that could be a set up for failure. Do something you enjoy; walking, exercise classes, and for some, yoga are forms of relaxation and exercise.

It's not unusual to have a loss of appetite during this time of grief and loss, especially as you are attempting to make sense of the addiction, however, you need the healthy calories to account for the energy you need to get through each day.

Andrew Weil, MD states "Human beings are literally fatheads. Fat accounts for about 60 percent of the dry weight of our brain. Omega-3 fatty acids optimize brain health. Because an omega-3 deficiency is common, and raising tissue levels of omega-3s has so many health benefits in general, I recommend that everyone take 2-4 grams of fish oil every day. I cannot emphasize the importance of this simple measure to improve emotional well-being."[6]

Make sure you're getting enough sleep. Lack of sleep over time affects your thinking and throws your metabolism out of balance. There are natural forms of sleep aids that you can take, be sure to talk to a pharmacist about this. When is the last time you had a physical, testing for a sexually transmitted disease (STD), a mammogram, and what about hormone testing? Progesterone is a natural anti-depressant for women, and stress can throw your cycles/ hormones out of balance. Talk to your doctor about it, put yourself on your to do list and prioritize your needs.

10. My list of to-do's, for me; because I deserve it and I am important. What do I need to do today in the short term to get to the long term goal? And what needs to happen in the intermediate to get there, i.e., my goal is to walk three times a week, long term. In the short term, I will sit down and figure out my schedule; in the intermediate, I will call my friend to see if she can watch the baby in order to get to my long term plan. This technique can go into the future as far as you want. It may be that five years from now you want your degree. What do

---

[6] Weil, Andrew MD. *Spontaneous Happiness.* (New York: Little, Brown and Company, 2011), 83.

you need to do now to make this happen, and in 2 1/2 years, where do you want to be with your plan? Plans don't always work out as we would like; be careful not to be hard on yourself if it does not take place as planned, just know that you did the best you could with what you have, and with the information/resources you have at hand.

My goal:
Short term
Intermediate
Long term

Managing Your Sexual Needs:

We are sexual beings. God created us with an innate need to be sexual. The Song of Solomon is a beautiful love story of a husband and wife who enjoyed each other's bodies and expressing intimacy with each other. Some partners have been made to feel shamed in this area of their lives. Shame-based thinking and identities may have come through family of origin, having parents that were non-communicative about sex, being sexually abused, or being in a relationship with a sex addict.

What's important for you is to know your limitations and boundaries around your need for intimacy. Your heart has been broken and it's not easy to open it up again. Things are different now; you may not have had sex since disclosure, or sometime before that. You've lost your trust and hope in the addict and the relationship, and also the ability to focus on the intimacy of what you thought you once had. The thought of being sexual/intimate with your spouse can be triggering. You may also be afraid of where he's been and who he's been with, and fear a sexually transmitted disease.

You also may be thinking that you are nowhere near the idea or thought of having sex with your spouse at this time. Know that you can choose to take all the time you need. If you are not ready, let your spouse know that you are not feeling safe emotionally or physically and are not yet able to go there. That is a boundary. You need time to trust the new behaviors and actions that he will be replacing for the old ones in his recovery program. If you are feeling pressured by your spouse to have sex, it should be something that you bring up in therapy with a therapist who is certified in sexual addiction. Some partners have told me they have sex with their husbands for fear of him acting out again. I understand, however, if he chooses to go there, you have no control of it. This is where a bottom line/plan or contract is in place, and polygraphs, which will come up later. For the most part, the men I have worked with are truly sorry and work their programs to gain their wives trust /families back.

With the partners I have worked with, flashes of images regarding the information they have, and what has been disclosed to them brings up disgust, anger, and hurt. Partners generally need to experience the time it takes to heal and process their spouses as someone who is safe, someone who is in recovery, and who can understand their needs and wounds. What I have found in working with couples who want to eventually be sexual again is a need to talk about the fear of what may come up for both of them. The partner fears that her husband will be thinking about the other encounters he's had, and he fears she is imagining him with someone other than herself; they're both experiencing the anxiety around the addiction. Some women report being fearful that if they do consent to having sex, it might set a precedent and the fear is that he may expect for things to go back to where they were. For others it may be that they are fearful of their own feelings that they may actually enjoy and want to be sexual, and yet still experience the anger and repulsiveness of his acting out behaviors.

It is normal to experience all of these thoughts and emotions. Once we start to talk about the fears and process them, they are not so scary. Boundaries and limits that have been talked about and set in place make a big difference for the couple. Most husbands are typically patient and understanding of their wives for wanting to leave lights on, keeping his eyes open, checking in from time to time with each other, and making sure their wives are feeling safe.

Sensate focus is a form of therapy that introduces practicing touching safely in a non-threatening way before you actually have sex. This is something you may bring up to your therapist. A great resource is *The Sexual Healing Journey,* by Wendy Maltz. Wendy is a certified sex therapist and provides help in the healing of relearning touch with techniques that offer opportunities to experience intimate touch that is safe and pleasurable. Cliff and Joyce Penner offer similar exercises and integrate a faith-based perspective into their work Restoring the Pleasure.

It's difficult to put a time frame on this part of the recovery. Each couple is unique and they seem to have a sense of knowing when the time is right, as time and recovery aligns itself.

John and Mariah walked into my office with the "afterglow," they could not wait to tell me, after one year of not having sex, that they were like two honeymooners. I asked if there was anything in particular they wanted to talk about today, they both blushed and told me how it "just happened." I have had couples tell me how they wept in each other's arms after a period of absence and reuniting their love in this way.

11. Define what sexual intimacy means to you.

| |
| |
| |
| |
| |

12. Write where you think you are in the process of being sexual with your husband and any limitations and fears you may have.

Managing your Spiritual needs:

"Seek first his kingdom and his righteousness, and all these things will be given to you as well." Matthew 6:33

This is my favorite verse. I surrender myself to a God that gives grace and healing. Without His strength I would not have been able to move through my journey and be where I am today. I initially questioned why God would allow this in my life. But I am also thankful for the things He's taught me about myself and showed me that I can be strong, set limits and boundaries when I lean on Him. This may not be the story for you. You may be questioning if there is a God, and why would he allow this horrific pain in your life. Something I know from reading scripture is that He hears you, and He wants to comfort you. He desires fellowship with you. Churches can be a place of healing, and support; but be cautious to put all your trust, faith, and expectations on people, places and things. God deserves that place more than anything—place or person. Spirituality is sacred and it is a personal relationship with a God who died for you. Scripture tells us that He knows every hair on our heads; He bottles every tear we've ever cried. Revelation 21:4 tells us that He will wipe away tears from all faces. This is the God who I seek and the One I trust who will never forsake me or leave me. He does not promise that I will have a picture perfect life, He promises to be there with me through the journey. It may not be where you are; don't judge yourself for this. If this is something you are interested in seeking, talk to the spiritual leaders in your community for help in finding a place where you might learn more about a personal relationship with God.

13. What is your relationship with God like? Can you trust Him with your heart, and what is one step you can do to hold unto this?

14. Can you draw a picture of what it might look like to trust God at His word? It might be of hands reaching out, allow your imagination to do the work.

Felt Sense

An awareness of our felt sense allows us to notice how our bodies react and orients itself to threatening as well as successful experiences. Having body awareness, and developing new strategies for survival mechanisms without shutting down or over reacting allows your body to organically start the process of completion from the body's response to triggers that activate the internal experience.

15. Draw an image of what it's like for you to be in your body when you're nervous system feels disrupted. Where in your body do you typically sense any distress?

Hope for the Heart

"Surely, I will deliver you for a good purpose: surely I will make your enemies plead with you in times of disaster and times of distress." Jeremiah 15:11

My challenge for today is:

Katie's Story

I thought I was going to die. My body was shaking and it just wouldn't stop. I could barely feel my heart beating. How could he do this to me? He is brilliant. He's been a great provider and great father. It felt surreal.

It began when he left his laptop open one night. I was about to close it for him and I saw the words on the screen that would change me forever. It was crystal clear that he was having an affair. I looked further and saw the pornography. Now I know why he wasn't having sex with me anymore. I began to wonder if I was good enough. What did those women have that I didn't? I broke down in tears every time the thoughts entered my mind.

Where do I go for help? I'm afraid of what people will think of me, and him, if I talk. My doctor checked my blood pressure and it was 190/115. I normally have a blood pressure reading of 130/75. I was hospitalized briefly while they got my blood pressure under control. I didn't want to rely on medicine for long. It was okay to take it for a while, but I wanted to try to do something else. I have three children. I didn't want them to grow up without a mother. One of the nurses referred me to a therapist who specialized in working with trauma. It wasn't long before I realized that I had just become a victim of trauma. I'm normally pretty strong willed, so I didn't want to remain a victim. I could barely get out of bed in the morning. Fortunately my employer was understanding and let me take the week off.

My therapist helped me understand the nature of trauma and PTSD. I was given a workbook that helped me through some of the grieving. I was able to get into a group for spouses of sex addicts that focused on healing our wounds. We didn't talk much about our husbands in the group. It was a safe place to heal. I continued to see my therapist outside of the group. She was trained in Eye Movement Desensitization Reprocessing (EMDR) and helped me manage the emotions and reactions so that I could get out of bed in the morning and stay focused on my work. I began to feel like I was becoming a mother again.

I also realized that the feelings I had were like things I felt as a child. I began to connect these feelings to the death of my grandfather when I was in eighth grade. I felt like he left me at that time. Feeling betrayed by my husband was bringing back bad memories. Over the next year, I stayed involved with my support group and continued my therapy. My husband has been working his program of recovery and healing. That helps some. We don't always connect, but it's helpful to know he is trying. We are getting to the point where we can try to work on our relationship. It's been a journey of healing wounds that I didn't know existed. There is hope.

When a physical wound heals it leaves a scar. Emotionally, I have been scarred. II still have memories and sometimes the hurt is overwhelming. The further I go, the less time it takes to bounce back. God is merciful, and I'm trying to let my scars remind me of his mercy. Some days it's harder than others. The memories will always be there. I have learned that there are ways to manage the pain and that the scars aren't the end of the journey.

    Katie

My Journal

My thoughts for today:

My feelings:

What am I sensing in my body?

Can I put any meaning to my experiences?

What can I be thankful for today?

Chapter 4

How Did I Get Into This Mess?

Part of the journey of healing will be to
consider how your wounds and family of
origin patterns contribute to the cycle.
(SOSA, p. 65)

My husband and I met and fell in love at the age of sixteen and eighteen. We were each other's
best friend, and spent as much time as we possibly could together between school and work. Both
of us are from large families, I am one of nine siblings, and my husband is one of seven. Our
parents did the best they could with what they had facing them, however, addiction was
prevalent in both families. Pornography, alcohol/drugs, sexual and physical abuse. We were
going to do things differently from our parents and communication was going to be our strength.
We spent hours talking about how to support one another, physically, and emotionally. For three
years we dated, and made major decisions together; where to go to college, how to spend our
money and save for our future. Once we got married, I supported him through college and we
started a family three years later.

Having children can put strain on a marriage, but we were determined to stay connected and
had our weekly date nights, occasional weekend get-a-ways, vacations, and supported each
other's thoughts and dreams. Sounds like a good plan for success, but the "secret" would rear its
ugly head now and then. A secret he had known since he was a child, finding playboy magazines
around the house made him feel good and he would get lost in the fantasy of what it would be like
to be loved and touched by the women in the magazine. As an adult, he would revert to the "good
feeling," the high-jacked brain, saturated with dopamine, the feel-good neurotransmitter, and
this became a pattern for him in times of high stress. He hid the magazines and the videos as
well. I was never aware of them; he hid them in our basement. Once technology came on board,
he figured out how to delete his history so I would not discover his well-kept secret.

I knew when things weren't right between us; there were certain behaviors that were not
congruent with the man I knew, like his anger towards God because life got hard, whether it was

our relationship, children, work, or finances. He with-drew, put up a wall that made communicating difficult, and had a short fuse. These were the times he was not reading his bible.

"What she doesn't know won't hurt her," was convincing for a time, and then the "shame tank." His conscious and the good man that he is at heart could not live with the double standard and hold unto the lies that the devil would feed him: You work hard, you deserve a little secret on the side, your wife is busy, she doesn't have time for you, she'll never know. The shame, remorse, and disparity he experienced was a hard secret to hold onto for so long, and hurtful to me/us led to periods of abstinence from any form of acting out. For many years he dabbled, and what was most hurtful to me were the times he "checked out." He wasn't with me. I did not experience his fully embodied self in the sacred space of our relationship. His acting out was not skin to skin, affairs, prostitutes, or escort services; and if this has been your experience with your spouse, or significant other, I am so sorry. That is another layer times ten. However, you may be able to relate to the emotional pain of the secret lies. I have had other women say that if pornography was the extent of the acting out, "the betrayal would not cut so deep." Absolutely. On the hand, I have also had women say they feel guilty because of what they're experiencing when other women have it so much worse. When the attachment bond in the most important adult relationship you've ever had is ruptured by the betrayal of sex addiction, it hurts at the very core of your being, regardless of what it looks like.

What got us started with the healing process was grieving the losses and facing the humiliation and shame in individual therapy. I knew he had to face the pain and betrayal of his own childhood wounds before he could move forward in putting off the old ways of coping. I, too, needed to look at patterns in my life that had any associations with family of origin. I was co-dependent, and to an addict, co-dependency fuels the obsession to have all their needs met by their spouses. I know now that I can never be all that to anyone, nor do I want to be.

My husband's motivation to go to meetings, therapy, and learn about sexual addiction meant a lot to me. More than that was the change of behavior, and understanding the impact and loss in our relationship. I did not want to be his therapist; I had my own healing to go through. His brokenness and falling on his knees for forgiveness was the beginning of the new man that now says, "I am sorry that I caused you so much pain." He has made things right with God and accepted His forgiveness, and I have forgiven him. He loves the Lord, and one of the special things in our relationship now is that we pray together. We struggled with this for many years, I believe it to be the shame that was there and made him uncomfortable.

Françoise

"One of the most difficult things spouses face, especially at the start of the journey, is being able to take their focus off the addict and begin to look inward." (SOSA, p.65)

1. Using the chart below, write down as many events in your life that you remember as an overwhelming experience

Stressful Event	Age	• What was most difficult in this event and how did you manage it? • Was there anyone, anything in particular that helped you?

What was your experience like in doing this exercise?

"One goal in your journey is to break the cycle in your life and in the lives of your children. This can be done even if your partner chooses not to get well." (SOSA, p.65)

2. As you look at your list of overwhelming events, can you see some of the events as issues that may keep you in a pattern that is destructive? Take the time to discern any associations that seem to have developed into a pattern, for example: an overwhelming event may be remembering Mom and Dad fighting at meal time, and it continued throughout your teens. In the present, as an adult, you struggle with sitting down and enjoying a meal with your family. A pattern of avoidance developed that now creates distance, not only with sitting down and enjoying your family at meals, but most times when the threat of discomfort comes up you find yourself getting busy with other things. It was a coping/protective mechanism that worked in the past, but for now in the present you avoid conflict, it brings up too much pain, particularly in this case around food/meals.

Past Event	Similarities in the Present

Is there anything you noticed about yourself while doing this exercise?

Abuse creates toxic shame—the feeling of being flawed and diminished and never measuring up. Toxic shame feels much worse than guilt. With guilt, you've done something wrong; but you can repair that; you can do something about it. With toxic shame there's something wrong with *you* and there's nothing you can do about it; you *are* inadequate and defective. Toxic shame is the core of the wounded child. This meditation sums up the ways that the wonderful child got wounded (Leo Booth/John Bradshaw).

MY NAME IS TOXIC SHAME

A pain that will not go away
I am the hunter that stalks you night and day
Every day everywhere

3. Is there any part of toxic shame that you can relate to?

| |
| |
| |
| |
| |
| |
| |
| |
| |
| |

S.H.A.M.E. = Self, Hatred, Accepting, My, Enslavement (SOSA, p.66)

4. Spend some time thinking about your "wounded child," what does that child need now, from you, the adult observer? Can you write a letter to your "inner child"? Some of the pain you may be experiencing now may feel like it felt as a child. Our bodies and minds remember and bear the burden of the trauma. Allow your adult self to give your wounded child the nurturing it needs. Take note of how old the wounded child is, as any images or thoughts come up. Also, notice if there are any association with any present experiences.

5. My wounded inner child:

Any revelations, thoughts or feelings you would like to journal about?

6. Circle any feelings you may have right now, and notice what the sensation is in your body. Jot it down next to the feeling.

Feeling List

angry		confused	
irritated		upset	
enraged		doubtful	
hostile		uncertain	
insulting		indecisive	
sore		perplexed	
annoyed		embarrassed	
upset		hesitant	
hateful		shy	
unpleasant		stupefied	
offensive		disillusioned	
bitter		unbelieving	
aggressive		skeptical	
resentful		distrustful	
inflamed		misgiving	
provoked		lost	
incensed		unsure	

infuriated	uneasy	
depressed	helpless	
lousy	incapable	
disappointed	alone	
discouraged	paralyzed	
ashamed	fatigued	
powerless	useless	
diminished	inferior	
guilty	vulnerable	
dissatisfied	empty	
miserable	forced	
detestable	hesitant	
repugnant	despair	
despicable	frustrated	
disgusting	distressed	
abominable	woeful	
terrible	pathetic	
despaired	tragic	
sulky	in a stew	

7. What is it like for you to be aware of how a feeling and sensation can be a response to how your body is experiencing stress and discomfort?

| |
| |
| |
| |
| |
| |
| |

"All families have them. But rarely are they ever spoken. You typically don't know they exist until you unknowingly break one of them." (SOSA, p.70)

8. What were some of the rules in your family of origin?

| |
| |
| |
| |
| |
| |
| |
| |

9. How did you know when you had broken a rule?

10. What were the results of breaking one of the family rules?

11. What are some of the family roles in your family of origin? And what role did you have? Who was who? (SOSA, p.74-78)

"These roles are developed to cope with family rules, trauma, and life in general."

| |
| |
| |
| |
| |
| |
| |
| |
| |
| |
| |
| |

12. Take a moment and look at your coping skills. Write down some of the things you have done to overcome some of your childhood wounds.

| |
| |
| |
| |
| |

---

13. The last few exercises may have been difficult for you. As a resource, use the space below to create an image of a safe place you have been or one you can imagine in your mind's eye that brings peace, love and joy to your heart. You may need to refer to this place occasionally when life feels overwhelming. Imagine it, feel it, use all of your senses to imprint the image in your brain.

Hope for the Heart

"For who is God besides the Lord? And who is the Rock except our God? It is God who arms me with strength and makes my way perfect. He makes my feet like the feet of a deer; he enables me to stand on the heights." Psalms 18:31-33

My challenge for today is:

Mia's Story

When I slowly began to come out of my shock, I was so mad at myself. How could this have happened to me? It is still so hard to believe. But I now accept that my husband's sex addiction is not about me. My dad was an alcoholic and he had cheated on my mother. I swore I would never marry an addict. My husband didn't drink or do drugs. He was a leader in our church. I thought surely I was safe by taking all the precautions I knew to marry a man that respected my values and principles. After all, we had met at a Christian college. We had gone on mission trips together in college and enjoyed our work in a service club. I thought I was doing things right. And now, I find myself married to a sex addict. I had never felt betrayed and violated at the extent of what this felt like. Life was a blur, and I lost my ability to function and make decisions as simple as what I needed for that day, for that moment. I was isolated from others and in shock.

After about six months of suffering alone, I went to a therapist who helped me understand that being married to a sex addict is traumatic. I began to see why I had been questioning my own reality. I began to learn how to feel again, and mostly for myself, the pain and grief I was experiencing. There was a lot of trauma and grief to heal from, and it hasn't been easy. After getting to a place where I could function again, and after I had been through a therapy group and a lot of trauma work, my therapist began to help me see some patterns that I had developed through the years, mainly the way I avoided conflict. With the help of my group therapy and therapist, I am now much more aware of how I shut down and am able to set limits.

Boundaries were a foreign concept in my family. I learned from my mother how to let people treat me like a doormat. She did the best she could. People have always taken advantage of me. I began to realize that it was almost sinful to say the dirty two letter word "no." When I got married, I was told to never say "no" to my husband. I just wanted to be a good wife, yet my main teacher had been my traumatized mother. I didn't realize she was traumatized until just recently. I then learned that addiction was in both of our family trees. The reason my husband never drank was that his grandparents were both alcoholics. He firmly believed that if he ever touched alcohol that he would lose control and become an alcoholic. Unfortunately he had been exposed to pornography at age eight, and he got hooked. He had a double life. I had no idea, and would've never suspected.

My therapist helped me define what clear boundaries were, and how to keep them. That was hard. I felt so wrong at first, but then I began to realize that I no longer felt resentment. I had been saying "yes" and becoming filled with hatred and bitterness. "No" was much more honest. I'm glad I got to a place where I could see some of the patterns in the family tree. I'm hoping to create a new legacy for my children. I don't know if my husband will get well or not. He is off to a good start. I have no control over him.

If someone had told me that my family had predisposed me to marrying a sex addict when I started this journey, I would not have believed it. I have met women who have told me that their therapist have told them they were sicker than their husbands, and that they had their own disease. After getting through the trauma and crisis, I was able to look into my own history and heal even more. I'm grateful that my current therapist saw things differently. I've had a journey of growth, and I know there is more to learn. Don't be afraid to look at your history after you heal from trauma. Let your wounds heal first, and then be open to where your journey can take you.

Mia

My Journal

My thoughts for today:

My feelings:

What am I sensing in my body?

Can I put any meaning to my experiences?

What can I be thankful for today?

Chapter 5

Spiritual Trauma: Has God Abandoned Me?

Definition for spiritual abuse: "Misuse and/or manipulation of the name of God and scripture, through position or teaching, in order to avoid consequences and project blame unto God." *(SOSA, p. 83.)*

I became a Christian and accepted the Lord as my Savior when I was twenty, a newlywed, and eager to learn God's principles and values for my life. My husband and I had the opportunity to go to Bible College and grow in our faith and knowledge of the word while leading bible studies, teaching Sunday school, attending a new church and being with like-minded friends who had a personal relationship with the Lord. This was all new to us, from what we had known and experienced growing up.

Becoming more Christ-like and spiritual-minded was very important to us as a couple, and regarding the way we raised our four children. The spiritual neglect in my marriage was having a husband who was not totally surrendered and angry with God when things did not go his way. When I noticed his pulling away from God I would question him and ask how his devotions were going, a question we had given each other permission to do for the sake of spiritual accountability

There was no evidence of a "man after God's own heart" for many years. He struggled with being the leader in our home, and this put a lot of stress on our relationship. I felt alone, and the shame of his acting out kept him at an emotional and spiritual distance. I wanted him to take the lead but he was not equipped for victory. He faced the battle alone and fearing the secret would be exposed, and the shame he experienced kept him from being honest with himself and accountable in our relationship.

Because I chose to work things out and he was willing to do what he needed to do to earn back my trust, we were able to move forward in our relationship. I've watched my husband transform his undisclosed life for a life that has set him free from the war of sexual addiction. He now leads me to the "living waters" in prayer, with a heart that is genuine and trusts God for all things in his life.

Françoise

Father Leo Booth writes:

"Religious addicts manipulate with guilt. Who dares to argue with the bible? Who dares not side with God? How can anyone object to a godly lifestyle? How can wanting your family to reap the rewards of heaven be abusive? When there is no balance, when religious addicts give their family no choice, when there is no room for differing opinions and beliefs, it becomes abuse. When they restrict their families lives, and continually trying to force them into a belief system under threat of rejection, punishment, or abandonment, it becomes abuse."[7]

1. Describe what spirituality means to you.

2. Has there been any spiritual abuse in your relationship? Can you describe it? And what has that experience been like for you?

---

[7] Booth, Father Leo. *When God Becomes A Drug*. G.P. Putnam's Sons, New York, 1991. P. 112.

"The addict might use shaming statements regarding care of the children, condition of the house, quality of meals and lack of frequent sex, to keep the spouse in isolation. When you feel that love and acceptance must be earned through good works, the sense of duty may drive you deeper into the same system. Breaking free becomes difficult because the fear of more isolation is devastating." (SOSA, p.86)

3. How does this quote resonate and have any experiential truth for you? How does it relate to any emotional or spiritual abuse in your past?

4. How does it make you feel and what are you experiencing?

My feelings about the abuse:
What I am experiencing is:

5. What can you do to break free from the "sense of duty" that may drive you deeper into the same system? What limits might you set for your own mental health and safety?

"Irrational demands for submission can keep spouses off balance in their relationships and their spiritual perspectives." (SOSA, p.85)

6. Have you been asked by the addict to do or go places out of your realm of comfort, and what has that been like for you? How have you responded?

7. Was the bible, God or scripture used to pressure and move you out of your comfort zone to participate in something that is uncomfortable and inappropriate? How did you respond?

"A study was conducted on women who had sought help from members of the clergy during times of trauma in their marriage. 71% reported dissatisfaction with the response of the clergy." (SOSA, p.88)

8. Circle any response that may have been given to you for advice:
   - Stay and works things out
   - Christians forgive and forget
   - Hope and pray for the best and God will change him
   - Try harder not to make him angry
   - He is hopeless and cruel but you are married to him
   - Cook better meals. Fix his favorite foods
   - Don't talk so much around him
   - All most men need is a warm dinner and a warm wife in bed
   - Wear him out with sex

9. What was your initial reaction to the advice? What do you think of it now?

"There isn't enough sex in the world to fill a hole that only God can fill."(SOSA, p.87)

As a spouse, no matter how hard you try, you can't fill the hole. The addict must assume responsibility for the choices he made in his sexually acting out behaviors.

Remember the three C's: you didn't *cause* it, you can't *control* it, and you can't *cure* it.

10. Can you put the three C's in your own words?

I didn't cause it; I can't control it; I can't cure it.

"Forgiveness is often presented as a simple choice. Unfortunately it runs deeper than a cognitive choice and it definitely isn't simple. Forgiveness is a process that doesn't need to take place quickly. It may be a 'one-day-at-a-time' process. It involves wrestling with difficult emotions and making difficult choices." (SOSA, p.91)

11. Forgiveness has been one of the most abused and misunderstood doctrines of Christianity. What does forgiveness mean to you? How have you been taught to understand forgiveness?

12. How has forgiveness been used to this point in your journey? Who has presented this concept to you? Pastors/Church Leaders? Friends? Family members?

13. What messages have you received about forgiveness from people in your life regarding the betrayal?

Dr. Janis Abrams Spring writes in her book, *How Can I Forgive You?*:

"Cheap forgiveness is a quick and easy pardon with no processing of emotion and no coming to terms with the injury. It's a compulsive, unconditional, unilateral attempt at peacemaking for which you ask nothing in return. When you refuse to forgive, you hold tenaciously to your anger. When you forgive cheaply, you simply let your anger go. Cheap forgiveness is dysfunctional because it creates an illusion of closeness when nothing has been faced or resolved, and the offender has done nothing to earn it."[8]

14. Can you identify with any part of "cheap forgiveness?"

---

[8] Springs, Janis Abrams, *How Can I Forgive You?*, (New York: Harper, 2004),15.

"Forgiveness is a choice that you will make when you are ready. It must not be approached quickly or with trite clichés. It is a conscious choice that you will make (more than once) to let go. It does not mean that you have to reconcile with the addict. Forgiveness and reconciliation are different. Forgiveness can take place without opening yourself up to being wounded repeatedly by an addict who chooses not to do the work of recovery and transformation. Reconciliation will involve hard work, which you probably aren't ready for at this time. Forgiveness isn't a one-time event. It may be a daily choice for a period of time. Having the pain of the past stirred up doesn't mean you haven't forgiven. It means that it hurts. Events of the past are stored on the hard drive of your brain. As healing takes place, the "down-time" from the wounds will lessen." (SOSA p. 91)

15. What has been the most difficult area of this journey for you to process? Is it the betrayal itself, trust, *forgiveness, or simply all of it?* It may be hard to put in words, it all feels and is very difficult. Can you lean into this without becoming overwhelmed? Start with one issue and see where you go from there. Practice self-care.

Process one aspect of the trauma at a time. It may be linked with other parts of your story. Stay with it long enough to know when you're out of your functional range and allow time to deactivate the negative energy you may be experiencing. Breathe.

16. Take time to notice what is going on inside of you. For now, notice if there is anything below that resonates with your personal experience.

I am in touch with my body and emotions and noticing:
I am identifying any internal or external anchors that will make me feel calmer and am noticing :
I am integrating a larger capacity to be in the here and now and noticing :
I am moving from the internal chaos to order and I am noticing:
I am organizing my thoughts and behaviors and I am noticing:

What do I notice now?

17. Have you short circuited your grief and trauma healing by forgiving before taking the time to process your wounds? What has that been like for you? And how is it working?

"One of my favorite TV shows is *All in the Family*. During one episode, Archie has had an emotional affair and Edith has discovered her husband's infidelity. As they are standing on the porch, Archie is begging for a second chance and says to Edith, 'Will you ever forgive me?' Edith replies that she had already made a decision to forgive, because if she didn't she would have to live with the bitterness and pain every day for the rest of her life. She then explains that her feelings are about the journey of rebuilding trust, dealing with the memories, and working on the marriage." (SOSA, p.92)

In *How Can I Forgive You?* Dr. Springs refers to "'genuine forgiveness' as a process that involves both the offender and the offended, which asks as much of the offender as it does of the hurt party. Offenders will learn how to perform bold, humble, heartfelt acts of repair to earn forgiveness, such as bearing witness to the pain they caused, delivering a meaningful apology, and taking responsibility for their offense. Hurt parties will learn to release their obsessive preoccupation with the injury, accept a fair share of responsibility for what went wrong and create oppor-tunities for the offender to make good."[9]

He may not have the capability to take on the full impact of the injury he's caused you; however, forgiveness is a very crucial part of your healing journey and your mental health. Don't rush into "cheap forgiveness."

Forgiveness does not infer that his behaviors are forgotten, as though this never happened. The consequences of the injuries will exist long after. Reconciling involves a lot of work. It's been eight years since disclosure for my husband and I, and it took a couple of years for me to get to genuine forgiveness. The initial consequences of his acting out and triggers left me feeling raw with the anger that I had to process, "If you ever do anything like this again, we are done." The fight was what I needed to stay in protective mode and hold to my limits and boundaries. It took a lot of energy to stay there. I wrestled with the difficult emotions. One of the many turning points for me was surrendering my anger and asking God to open my eyes and heart, and allow me to see the new man he was becoming. At that point I knew I was ready to start the process of taking my armor off and start trusting him with my heart again, in tiny bite pieces, one at time.

You may not want to go anywhere near forgiveness at this time. The addict may not be taking responsibility for reconciliation and ownership for his actions. Amy's husband went to prison and she was left to manage her pain and the responsibility of the children on her own. She was left alone to reorganize her life. She experienced every emotion you can imagine, including missing him. A year later and divorced, Amy was able to let go of her dream with the man she loved. Letting go and forgiving are never easy.

---

[9] Springs, Janis Abrahms. *How Can I Forgive You?* Harper: 2004, p. 15.

18. Can you define what forgiveness means to you?

19. Do you think you are anywhere near "genuine forgiveness?" Why or why not?

20. Wherever you are in the process of forgiveness, give yourself permission to be alright with it. What you don't want and need is "cheap forgiveness" which is a quick and easy pardon with no processing of emotion and no coming to terms with the injury. Take your time. Take a moment and write out how you feel about the forgiveness process.

Hope for the Heart

"I love the Lord, because He heard my voice; he heard my cry for mercy. Because he turned his ear to me, I will call on him as long as I live." Psalms 116:1, 2

My challenge for today is:

Marianne's Story

I barely remember stumbling into my pastor's office. I had nowhere to go so I went to him. My body was shaking and I could hardly get words out of my mouth. He tried to calm me down. I couldn't get over the shock and pain. It was hard to breathe. The pictures were all over our computer. How could he do this to me? All of the pictures were gross. They kept coming at me and I finally had to unplug the computer from the wall to get them to stop.

"Please try to calm down—I'd like to understand what is going on," he said.

Then the pastor asked me about my relationship with my husband. Did I respect and honor him the way the bible teaches? "I guess so; though I'm sure I could do better" was my reply. I felt confused.

"I know your husband has the weight of the world on his shoulders. Trying to provide for you and the kids isn't easy," said the pastor. But the pictures were so horrible. I had never seen anything like them. I couldn't get them out of my mind. I continued to share my pain through many tears. I was so upset. My husband has always been involved with the church. A man who loves his wife and kids wouldn't watch pornography, or so I thought. I felt nauseated.

The next thing the pastor said confused me. He wanted to know if I had been reading my bible and praying each day. I told him that I did my best, but that I'm sure I could do better. I asked him if he thought that God was punishing me for not having enough quiet times. His answer was "you never know." He then opened a bible and started talking to me about submission to my husband and respecting him as the leader of our home. I didn't know what to say. I came to him for help as a man of God.

The next thing that happened made my heart sink into my stomach. He told me I needed to make sure that I dressed in clothes that would attract my husband and that I should make sure that I "don't deprive him" of what he really needs. And of course, he had a bible verse to back this up. He told me to try to be the best wife I could be and make the house nice and neat and that this would keep my husband from looking at naked women. If I found him looking at pornography I was to have more sex with him and make him want me more than all of those other women. I couldn't be like them. They were young and vibrant, and I had given birth to three children.

The last thing he did left me so depressed. He said that I couldn't teach my Sunday school class or be a leader in the children's ministry because it might hurt the church if someone found out. I thanked the pastor for seeing me and left.

When I got home I was so full of shame. It felt like it was my fault and that if I had been right with God, my husband wouldn't be looking at other women. Was God punishing me for something? I loved my work with the children, and now I didn't have that anymore. I couldn't even turn to God when I needed him the most. That next Sunday it took all of my energy to get my children ready for church. It felt like I could barely crawl to the back pew, I was so embarrassed. It felt like everyone in the auditorium knew and was looking right at me. I tried to keep my head up for the kids. I couldn't take much more.

It was about three years later when I read a book about spiritual abuse. Not from cult groups or weirdoes, but from typical churches. It wasn't intentional, but the damage to people's faith was gigantic. I realized I had looked to my pastor as the voice of God. He was a broken human being just like the rest of us. He wanted to help, but knew nothing about the problems I brought to him. I had to realize that he was a human, and God was God. I began to see how God and the bible could really help me, but if they were used wrong, it would destroy me. God didn't want me to pretend nothing had happened. I needed to address these problems with my husband directly. I went to a church elder who had helped people through these problems before. He gently showed me where the pastor had used the bible verses out of context and that they didn't mean anything close to what was taught. He then said that I didn't need to jump in and get involved in activities until I felt ready, and that the church needed to be a safe place for me to heal and grow. Whenever I wanted to get involved I could let him or others know and they would help me at that time. For the first time in years, someone could open a bible and use it to help me heal, not shame me.

I read a book called Letters to a Devastated Christian *by Gene Edwards. At the end of the book, it makes a suggestion that I found difficult, but it's proven to be true. It encourages a return to a church family. Strangely, the place where I was so hurt became a place of hope and healing. I had to find a healthier church family, but once I did, it became a great place to be. I wish all churches could be like mine. If you are struggling, the problem isn't God. It's the imperfect humans in churches. Be careful, but don't give up. I found that God could still work through some of those broken people to help me, my children, and even my husband get to a better place.*

Marianne

My Journal

My thoughts for today:

My feelings:

What am I sensing in my body?

Can I put any meaning to my experiences?

What can I be thankful for today?

Chapter 6

Myths of the Journey

Marriage is often a journey that people begin with fairy-tale expectations. However, the honeymoon ends when the myths are exposed and reality sets in. (SOSA, p. 94)

It sometimes seems easier to say, I'm done; I've had enough. How much more can I take of this? The triggers send you into orbit leaving you with an over activated and anxious nervous system, always looking over your shoulders and waiting for the other shoe to drop. You start to doubt your own ability to keep your emotions regulated and a sense of coherence. You may wonder if divorce is the best option. The triggers feel like bits and pieces of another disclosure that rips your heart out. Your body starts to settle and trust that he is in recovery, and you discover more information, more infidelities, or see him looking at attractive women and think that there must be something wrong with you; you're not pretty enough, you can't measure up. The fear is driven by a sense of false hope; if I do this, or if only I could be more like that; and may leave you with self-loathing thoughts such as; this is my fault or I am not good enough.

And there are the children, financial needs, a dream of growing old together, and the energy goes back into restoring the last slip, hoping it won't be a full blown relapse. You try harder than ever and make sure he's going to all his meetings, therapy, and talking to his sponsor. He tells you to stay "on your side of the street" and you feel rejected, hurt and wounded that he is not communicating with you, and you so need to know he is working his program.

That's a lot of energy. The truth is that it's not your responsibility to make sure he's working his recovery program. But it's his responsibility to make sure you feel safe by working his program. I remember being told "you stay on your side of the street." It nearly threw me over the edge. Really? So he's acting out and I'm not supposed to do anything about it?

There are things you do need to do to take care of yourself. That's why boundaries are important to set up for your security and the safety of your heart and life. Partners have a tendency to get stuck in their needs and limits and the follow through of the consequences. The "what to-do" if he does not follow through with the boundaries. The follow through is important, integrity is the glue in consistency. It takes energy to keep to your word and it takes as much when you don't.

Think of how you feel about yourself when you look the other way, minimize, and rationalize a principle that you value, and hold so close to your heart. This is not to say that youbecome a private investigator. Be the soul keeper of your heart. Your words and thoughts are meaningful. Your responsibility is to take care of yourself, your needs list, your limitations, and your bottom line.

Françoise

Myth 1

"This wouldn't have happened if I'd been a better spouse."

Have you bought into this lie? Why?
What do you believe about this myth?
Lies:
Truth:

Myth 2

"We must not be right for each other."

Have you bought into this lie? Why?
What do you believe about this myth?
Lies:
Truth:

Myth 3

"My spouse doesn't want sex with me because I'm not attractive enough."

Have you bought into this lie? Why?

What do you believe about this myth?

Lies:

Truth:

Myth 4

"My spouse won't need to go somewhere else for sex if I become more sexual and do whatever he/she wants."

Have you bought into this lie? Why?
What do you believe about this myth?
Lies:
Truth:

Myth 5

"Everything will be fine if we throw ourselves into the marriage."

Have you bought into this lie? Why?
What do you believe about this myth?
Lies:
Truth:

Myth 6

"I can fix whatever is wrong with my spouse."

Have you bought into this lie? Why?
What do you believe about this myth?
Lies:
Truth:

Myth 7

"I am worthless if my spouse does not approve of me and accept me."

Have you bought into this lie? Why?

What do you believe about this myth?

Lies:

Truth:

Myth 8

"I'll be a failure if I get a divorce."

Have you bought into this lie? Why?

What do you believe about this myth?

Lies:

Truth:

Myth 9

"I need to know every detail of what my partner has done to trust again."

Have you bought into this lie? Why?
What do you believe about this myth?
Lies:
Truth:

Myth 10

"Just looking at pornography isn't really adultery."

Have you bought into this lie? Why?
What do you believe about this myth?
Lies:
Truth:

Myth 11

"It's not biblical to abstain from sex with your spouse."

Have you bought into this lie? Why?

What do you believe about this myth?

Lies:

Truth:

Myth 12

"Obedience to God will keep me from experiencing the pain."

Have you bought into this lie? Why?
What do you believe about this myth?
Lies:
Truth:

Myth 13

"Only the addict should go to counseling."

Have you bought into this lie? Why?

What do you believe about this myth?

Lies:

Truth:

Myth 14

"Time heals all wounds."

Have you bought into this lie? Why?
What do you believe about this myth?
Lies:
Truth:

Myth 15

"Recovery happens when the addict is delivered and the spouse forgives and gets past the hurt."

Have you bought into this lie? Why?
What do you believe about this myth?
Lies:
Truth:

1. Were there any of the myths that were especially difficult for you? What about it made it difficult?

2. Notice what you are experiencing and feeling. See if you can make any meaning of it.

Hope for the Heart

"His mouth is full of lies and threats; trouble and evil are under his tongue. He lies in wait near the villages; from ambush he murders the innocent. His eyes watch in secret for his victims; like a lion in cover he lies in wait. He lies in wait to catch the helpless; he catches the helpless and drags them off in his net." Psalms 10:7-9

My challenge for today is:

Heidi's Story

Which way is up? I found myself wondering helplessly as reality hit hard. How could this not be about me? Everything is a giant question mark. I keep reading that "the addiction isn't about me," but that doesn't make it feel better. It sounds like it makes sense, but I'm not sure of anything right now.

It's taken several months to get through the shock. Now that I'm in a better place, I'm really questioning some of the advice I got earlier. When I shared with my best friend Sherry, she was helpful and listened whenever I needed her. I leaned on her a lot those first few weeks. Then things began to change in subtle way. Over coffee one morning, Sherry seemed to imply that I might have caused the problem. She asked about my sex life. I told her that my husband wanted it, but I just hadn't felt like it since discovering the pornography. It just didn't feel safe.

I wondered if it was really about him. I went to talk to a counselor. He told me he was a biblical counselor with a credential from a major Christian Counseling Association. Jim [name changed] claimed he was trained in sexual addiction. He opened the bible and started talking about "not depriving my husband" from 1 Corinthians 7. When I talked about how frightened I was, Jim told me to "trust God and try harder."

Off to the gym I went. Time to lose twenty pounds and make myself more attractive. It made me more depressed. How could I keep up with these young girls? After giving birth to three children and being forty-four years old, how could I ever be as attractive as the women my husband seemed to want so desperately? After all, he was willing to risk his job, health, marriage, and family. I tried everything I could think of, yet the depression and emptiness just got worse.

I finally found a professional counselor (who was also Christian) who was really trained in treating sex addicts and their families. I had to drive two hundred miles, but it was worth it. This really wasn't my fault. My husband's problem began when he was first exposed to pornography at age eight. He brought the problem into our marriage. I began to realize I had believed the lies. Pastors, biblical/nouthetic counselors were trying to make me believe that these problems wouldn't have happened if I had been a better wife and had more faith.

Don't buy the lies! I now help with a support group for spouses of sex addicts. My wounds needed to heal. I had to take that time for me. I realized that the advice I got early in this nightmare of a journey had been wrong. Not only wrong—it was abusive and traumatic. I thought I was safe, and yet I ended up getting hurt even more. I'm grateful to my current therapist and support group. They help keep me focused on my healing, and I no longer believe the lies.

Heidi

My Journal

My thoughts for today:

My feelings:

What am I sensing in my body?

Can I put any meaning to my experiences?

What can I be thankful for today?

Chapter 7

To Tell or Not To Tell: The Disclosure Dilemma

Regardless of how you found out, it was one of the most shocking, devastating and painful things you have ever discovered. (SOSA, p. 104)

Disclosure is a necessary part of your healing process. My husband and I did not have a formal disclosure. The secret and information was revealed when it was discovered; when he got caught. It would have been better with the help of a professional in a timely manner. Something I now wish we had done. I believe it's a symbolic moment for a couple and gives hope that is so desperately needed for the partner to move forward, regardless of whatever her decision is. A formal disclosure entails a time of preparing both partner and addict. The addict is given an assignment to go over the timeline of sexual acting out behaviors, without adding unnecessary details that may trigger his partner in the future.

Partners are extremely curious, wanting information about the places the addict has been, gifts they have purchased, how money has been spent, and has he been with anyone they know? How many prostitutes they have been with? Did they ever want to leave her for any one of the affairs?

These are all valid concerns. Putting together a list of questions going over them with a trained therapist is helpful. It allows you to check in with how this information may or may not be helpful in terms of the future and how it may linger in your thoughts and cause more emotional pain.

Partners may be given a form with questions such as, what is your bottom line? And what is your worst fear? The questions are integrated in the disclosure, as well as any concerns you may have. My therapist was not a certified sexual addiction specialist. She supported and had empathy for me. Neither of us had any idea at the time that a formal disclosure would have been helpful and an integral part of the process of healing and validation for the partner. It would have eliminated the fear of the unknown.

I questioned if there were any other parts to his secrets. I wondered if he had betrayed me in any other ways. I asked many questions, wanted assurance over and over, threatened that if he was not telling me the whole truth I would leave him. He assured me over and over that there were no more secrets to be told, as much and as often as I needed to hear this. It was not easy to believe, I had one foot in the door and one foot out. I was guarded and protected in my position, and fearful of letting my guard down lest he think that I was not going to hold true to my word. I have added a list of questions below that are important to address.

In my experience with the partners and formal disclosures, the partner needs her therapist as an advocate and support. Part of the work with the partner is to make sure she has the time she needs to process the information during the disclosure. One woman I worked with stated during the disclosure, "You mean you were doing this while I was in infertility treatment?" She was putting the time line together, and could not get past this point. I needed to slow things down for her and allow her to have her questions to get through the entire disclosure. For the addict, there is relief when the disclosure is over due to the extreme level of anxiety around preparing for it. They may be fearful and anxious, and simply just want to get through this in a hurry. You need to know this is for you and to take the time you need to get through it.

Françoise

"The moment of disclosure/discovery of your spouse's sexual addiction places the two of you at radically different places. Beginning the process of recovery takes the couple through a journey of conflict, confusion, and chaos. It's difficult for a couple to navigate, and professional help is almost always required." (SOSA, p.105)

1. If you have had a formal disclosure, what was it like for you, and leading up to it?

| |
| |
| |
| |
| |

2. If you have not had a formal disclosure, what was "discovery" like for you?

| |
| |
| |
| |
| |

If you have not had a "formal disclosure," I suggest that you bring this up in group, talk to those who have experienced one, pray about it, and find a therapist that is a certified sexual addiction specialist that believes in the trauma model. You can search places such as "The Association of Partners of Sex Addicts Trauma Specialists (www.partnertraumaspecialists.org) or the International Association of Certified Christian Sexual Addiction Specialists (www.sexaddictioncertification.org).

One of the hardest things to go through without the formality of the formal disclosure process is the dribbling effect. This is where bits and pieces of new information are disclosed over time. It is possible that the addict has forgotten some of the information, some of the information may date back many years. The dribbling effect can be debilitating and re-traumatizing. A well planned disclosure, given enough time, that the addict is ready to be open and vulnerable and willing to take a polygraph to ensure his level of honesty, makes a huge difference for partners. In terms of your self-care after the disclosure, make sure to have a plan in place. Plan to be with someone that is a support/resource to you, drive in separate cars, have someone watch the children, and a scheduled meeting with your therapist soon after or right after the session. I prefer to do this right after the disclosure. It's a time to sort out and help you manage what is going on for you, and allow any new information to be processed.

Consider the following questions which reinforce that indeed you are not asking for too much by requesting a disclosure.

- Does your spouse have unaccountable time or money?
- Does your spouse have unexplainable moods?
- Does your spouse's mood depend on whether he or she gets sex or not?
- Does your spouse have a lack of sexual activity with you?
- Does your spouse have a history of emotional, physical or sexual abuse or neglect?
- Does your spouse have a supply of pornography (especially the kind you get at adult bookstores or download from the internet)?
- Is there a lot of anger or erratic behavior when you say "no" to your spouse sexually?
- Do you feel alone during your sexual encounters or in your relationship?
- Do you feel used, dirty, or abandoned after sexual encounters?
- Is there a sense that your spouse got his or her "fix" and is now better?
- Has your spouse made promises to quit a behavior and failed?
- Does your spouse have what looks like a double life?[10]

---

[10] http://www.sexaddict.com/HusAddict.html. Used with permission from Dr. Douglas Weiss

3. Information you would want to know for yourself protection:

4. Is there anything you do not want to know?

5. What are your greatest fears?

6. How much do you already know about his acting out?

| |
| |
| |
| |
| |

7. What is your bottom line?

| |
| |
| |
| |
| |

8. With your therapist, develop a list of questions that you want answered;

- What is the nature of the acting out? For example; extramarital affairs, prostitution, pornography, strip clubs, voyeurism, or masturbation.
- When did these behaviors start regarding our relationship?
- What is the time frame of the addictive behaviors?
- How often and how long have these behaviors occurred?
- Will this acting out behavior affect my health?
- Where did this behavior take place?
- How much money have you spent engaging in these behaviors?
- How has this money been acquired?

- What do I need to know regarding these places or people, have these behaviors been with any friends, family members or anyone I may be in contact with?
- Are there any legal issues that I should know about?
- Any behaviors that resulted in a pregnancy or abortion?
- Any sexual behaviors with minors?
- Was there any contraction of a sexually transmitted disease? Have you been tested for STD's?
- Was the acting out heterosexual or did it involve same-sex activity?

Some of these questions are incorporated in his disclosure. Jot down anything that comes to your mind and go over these with your therapist. Use more paper if needed. Knowing all the details is not in your best interest, such as hair color, perfume etc. Let a qualified professional guide you through the process.

9. Jot down a list of questions that are important to you, and why you think knowing this information would be helpful to you.

During a formal disclosure, if there is something that is not clear, and you sense yourself shutting down, or highly upset, slow it down with the help of your therapist. Let your therapist know beforehand what might be helpful for your comfort level. There are times I've moved closer to the partner and put my hands on her shoulders, a way of supporting her. Ask for clarification if you need it; take a break. Breathe. I generally plan a two-hour session and a one-hour session for the partner afterward. Remember this is for you. You will need time to process this information. I find that the partners typically have questions in the aftermath of the disclosure, and their spouse is reluctant to attend another session. "We have been through this, and I don't want to reopen this." Most partners I've worked with believe they have a pretty solid idea of what will be divulged, however, hearing what might be your worst scenario, or anything new, throws another layer of trauma to your system and needed time for the new information to settle before you revisit this. If this is the case, ask for another meeting with specific questions to any new information, with the help of your counselor. Lynn was so afraid of shutting down during the session that she wrote down all of her spouse's answers. For Lynn, this was a means of staying in the moment. This is where the therapist/client relationship is helpful. She/he will know when to slow things down, when you are detaching and possibly disengaging from the here and now.

In the aftermath of the disclosure you may want to discuss an abstinence contract for your own security and safety. Most specialists in this field recommend a forty to ninety day abstinence plan. For the addict, abstinence is therapeutic processes that can neurochemically reset the brain. Abstinence challenges some of the core beliefs of a sex addict. Initially, the addict's ongoing recovery is a priority. This can be difficult for partners to accept. It takes a chunk of their week. Family and household responsibilities are put on hold. They have meetings. Some may go to as many as three per week, and others do a 90/90 (ninety meetings in ninety days). Finding a right match with a sponsor/accountability person gives the addict the opportunity to report any sexual behaviors of any kind. The first few months are a jump start to a healthy recovery program. There are also inpatient treatment centers all over the country that serve as a great purpose for healing, in a manner of psycho-education, psychotherapy, and address the needs of family and couples work. Another option is an intense couple's weekend. It can get intense. I remember Anna and Mark, after arriving Friday afternoon ready to pack their bags by Saturday morning. Things had gotten so out of control for them, they could not imagine being together another day, and by the end of the weekend this couple left holding hands. In their aftercare couples group, they promoted the workshop as a necessity for the healing that needs to take place in the couples work. These workshops go on for men as well, without the partner.

Some couples contract to do an in-house or out-of-house separation for a period of time. The in house can be tricky, finances dictate the necessity. It is doable in separate rooms and a plan for minimal contact and communication while seeing a therapist. It is more complex when there are children involved. There is a form/contract at the end of this chapter that may help with some idea of what to expect.

In addition to the contract you may want to implement what you need to be safe; a security program on the computer, meetings, sponsor, individual therapy, couples therapy. You might request a weekly check-in that includes sharing emotions, positive affirmation, needs, ownership and an update on sobriety. This tool takes the place of thinking that you have to be the one to continually ask about his sobriety and playing the detective. Knowing that you can do SOBERS on a weekly basis and alleviates some of the pressure you may have to be overinvolved.

Safe – Am I feeling safe with you right now and how do I know it?

Ownership – Can I own the thoughts and feelings I'm sharing with you

Behavior – Have I been respectful and loving this week?

Engaged – Have I been engaged in my recovery program and do I need to do something different?

Responsibility – What do I need to take responsibility for? Something I've done or something I've neglected?

S –Sobriety date

We will address more of these suggestions later when we refer to your needs list.

I mentioned a polygraph as a tool that is implemented with the disclosure. This generally is done just before the disclosure, and every three to six months thereafter for an agreed upon time. This too, can be written up in the contract for your emotional safety.

Barbara Steffens, in her book, "Your Sexually Addicted Spouse," page 71, reports that, "partners seek truth, not control, though many fail to understand this. A partner's motivation for truth stems from the need to once again feel safe, to keep the environment safe. But the use of polygraphs remains controversial in many people's mind. Yet even though they cannot be deemed 100 percent fail-safe, police departments and prison systems continue to use them, because they provide the best technology available to decipher fact from fiction. As for partners of sex addicts, the polygraphs can play a huge role in establishing a foundation of truth on which to begin to build a new marriage based on honesty and a slow-growing sense of trust."

The article written on the following page by Fred Hunter, a polygraph expert, is keenly aware and sensitive to the partners' needs. He takes time to answer questions, and validate the fear partners have. I was really impressed with Fred, after asking him to read Barbara's book, in order to give him insight into what the partner is going through. He thanked me for the insightful resource that gave him the ability to have a deeper understanding of what the partner is experiencing.

I had one partner say to me, "He really gets it. He gave me the time I needed to go over my questions, and validated my fears." So make sure they get the "he gets it," and have an understanding of the trauma model.

A polygraph is a verification that provides the assurance the partner needs. Ask for what you want, you do not have to be the one that researches this information. However, you want to know that the examination is provided by an expert who is familiar with sex addiction.

THE USE OF POLYGRAPH TESTING DURING A SEXUAL HISTORY DISCLOSURE

by Fred L. Hunter

The use of the sexual history by a therapist is the primary tool during counseling intake in evaluating secret sexual behaviors so destructive to the very core of any relationship or marriage between partners.

In most cases these secret sexual behaviors have been in play long before partners became one. However, they often escalate over time during relationships for a variety of reasons.

It is imperative for the therapist and then the unoffending partner to understand such medicating behaviors and their escalation. It is not unusual for those using masturbation to pornographic/lustful images to escalate to more dangerous voyeuristic behaviors or interactions with others which then ultimately lead to sexual contacts outside of a relationship.

Success in a client's recovery is paramount on their being truthful and accountable for their actions so that appropriate counseling and boundaries can be established.

However, truth often takes a back seat to fear. As a result, the client lies or minimizes their secret sexual behaviors and spends time stuck in denial and the fear of unknown consequences. This denial then undermines their credibility further with their partner as well as delays proper or affective treatment.

It is a reality of such addiction type counseling that fear will dominate both partners. The offending partner is fearful of the consequences of their actions (divorce, rejection, being cut off from their friends and family, hurting their partners more, etc.). The unoffending partner reacts further from the offenses admitted because of lies and manipulations from the past and investigative process often leading to counseling which then drive their fear of the unknown (divorce, not being worthy, getting a STD, losing the family unit, etc.).

Polygraph can play a unique role in this process after a therapist develops a sexual history with the client. Its use then shifts from a denial breaker (which it often is) to a tool of therapeutic evaluation to ensure that a full and complete disclosure has been made. Then and only then can a therapist be sure as to the behaviors they are treating and the establishment of realistic sobriety boundaries.

An important side bar to this therapeutic evaluation is that it also adds clarity to deal with the fear created by the infidelity process within the unoffending partner.

By the therapeutic utilization, setbacks to counsel because of denial and lying can be prevented. Further disclosures of inappropriate behaviors coming after a disclosure is made and reconciliation is attempted is disastrous. A client will only get so many chances at reconciliation before the unoffending partner steps away. Therefore the offending partner must be truthful, show remorse, and be accountable or their chances of reconciliation are often doomed.

The basic thrust of a sexual history polygraph evaluation is to identify and clarify sexual interactions with others beside the unoffending partner (men, women, and children). This is crucial even when only inappropriate behaviors (pornography, voyeurism, masturbation, exposure, internet interactions, secret non-sexual relationships with others, etc.) short of sexual contact have been admitted. Not only is denial about contact with others often the norm for a lying offending partner, it will also be the worst case fear of the unoffending partner whether voiced or not.

Unoffending partners should be inventoried about what their concerns may be about their partner. Suggesting possible polygraph testing areas is a subtle way to identify them. Most unoffending partners may have pages of such questions; however it is the fear themes that dominate their questions which is revealing. This too can be a way of identifying areas for counsel as well for the unoffending partner.

Proper polygraph technique will only allow 3 to 5 relevant test questions depending on the examiner involved, and is also why the thrust at this point is to sexual contact with others. However fear of contact with prostitutes, co-workers, neighbors, relatives, or social acquaintances often surface and may need to be addressed.

If a number of questions persist with the unoffending partner, then additional testing may be suggested.

Sexual history disclosure polygraph testing protocol dictates the results should go first to the therapist. In this way the offending partner will have safety to discuss untruthful test results with the therapist in an effort to resolve areas of denial. This protocol then also does not set back the unoffending partner further with deceptive results. Once the therapist is satisfied that the offending partner's disclosure is accurate, then a disclosure and reconciliation can be made with the unoffending partner.

Therapists seeking to learn more about polygraph testing for sexual disclosure should contact those therapists who use such a tool in their practice for further insight. Also the American Polygraph Association web site can provide information on the suggested required testing protocol (PSCOT certification) necessary for such evaluations.

Further polygraph testing after the initial sexual history process is conducted to ensure that the offending partner is being truthful in maintaining their sobriety boundaries. Again the protocol is that results would first go to the therapist. Information as to violations or erosion of sobriety boundaries is then the offending partner's home work with his therapist for the next few sessions. In this manner, slips in the recovery process can be minimized, but also dealt with immediately to ensure total relapses back to previous destructive behaviors or sexual contact with others do not occur.

The continuing fears of the unoffending partner will also be an issue of review prior to such future tests after the sexual history. The idea being that the unoffending partner can reconcile with accountability while the offending partner re-establishes credibility with good polygraph results in the recovery process.

However, attention must be made to the unoffending partner's concerns as the recovery process moves forward.

"In no way does this put blame on you for the action of your partner. You are not responsible for them. Only for how you choose to react and cope." (SOSA, p.114)

If you decide to do an in-house or out-of-house separation, what will you need, what kind of time frame do you want to agree on, what kind of parameters based on some of the options that have already been mentioned might be something to explore.

When Lisa was asked what her needs list was, she reported, "I need for him to be honest and loyal to me as he vowed to me on our wedding day." That is the overall bottom line. As time went on, Lisa was able to be specific about what she wanted. She started with a list of needs that triggered her fears and activation that left her feeling out of control. She identified her specific triggers, i.e., when her husband traveled, she needed to know what his plan was for maintaining his sobriety. Lisa felt that if she was not sexual with her husband, he would seek it somewhere else. She wanted to be intimate, however, in a way that would promote "safe non-sexual touch." She defined what that meant to her, and felt that a three month sabbatical would give her what she needed to regain her sense of safety around this issue. For the addict, the sabbatical is a form of rewiring the physical and psychological urges that the addict is addicted to. In the process of the sabbatical, attunement to their bodies and minds cultivates an awareness and reality of why and when the need for a coping mechanism got started.

Write out some of the parameters/conditions that you would like to set in place, regardless of how you work out the living situation. In general, just to mention a couple, computers and movies. Patricia reported that she was not comfortable watching movies with her husband. This was something they had always enjoyed doing together. It triggered her losses and sense of safety.

Triggers:	Needs List:

10. What are some of your thoughts regarding a separation, whether it's in-house or out? What are your fears?

| |
| |
| |
| |
| |
| |
| |
| |
| |

11. What are the conditions for getting back together?

| |
| |
| |
| |
| |
| |
| |

Contract

This contract is designed to assist you in achieving and maintaining positive changes in your relationship. By making a commitment and putting it in writing, as well as consequences for not following through you are actively taking steps toward healing the trust that has been violated.

I, _____, agree to make every effort possible to make the following change(s) at my partner's request. I understand that this change is very important to my partner and therefore also very important to me. This contract will continue throughout treatment unless a new contract is made, or until one or both parties decides to end the relationship.

The contract I agree to is:

Name: _____ Date: _____
    Husband or Wife

Name: _____ Date: _____
    Witness

12. If this applies, this exercise is for your spouse to write a letter to himself, as though you are writing it. You may want to let him know he has a couple of weeks from the time he agrees to write it and that you would like to have it read to you in a couple's therapy session. However, it may also be just as successful do this on your own.

The letter is about him getting it—getting what it's been like for you to live with an addict, getting into your feelings, such as fear, anger, loneliness, disappointment, and the betrayal. He may or may not want to participate; however, I find this exercise healing for the wounded couples. The partner experiences the validation that is long overdue for her feelings and what she's been through. If it's not close to what the experience has been like, ask your spouse to rewrite it based on the parts of the letter that are not accurate. He may get some of your pain, but it's also important that he understands from your perspective, as best as he can. This is not about shaming the addict; in fact, it can be healing for him. I found that the exercise gives the addict permission without the fear of the shame holding him back to honestly and publically tell you how truly sorry he is for what you are going through. And as you see, for Nina it was exactly what she needed.

A sample of a letter that Jay wrote as if his wife, Nina, were writing it:

"Thank you Jay, thank you. Thank you for taking something, the one relationship that was beautiful in my life, and making it sinister. Thank you for being just another part of the whole that tells me I'm not good enough, that I'm broken, different, and less than what you want. Thank you for affirming that I don't deserve to be happy, that no matter what I do, I am meant to be treated like crap by the world, and that I'm intrinsically worthless and unwanted, even by those who are supposed to adore me.

All I wanted was you. All I wanted was to be with you Jay, to share life together, to give and receive genuine love, passion and affection. I didn't need perfection, I didn't need the world. I needed you. And instead of that, I got _____. I got to feel crazy and stupid as you talked your way into circles to escape from taking responsibility for your actions. I got to feel worthless and unwanted while you disconnected from the world. I got to feel marginalized, forgotten and unwanted. Did I mention unwanted?"

Jay "got it" and Nina's comment after the letter was, "I could not have written it any differently." She needed to know he understood her pain. She felt validated, heard, and understood.

Any thoughts on this exercise? If you have been through this, are you willing to share what it was like for you?

Hope for the Heart

"Unless the Lord builds the house, its builders labor in vain. Unless the Lord watches over the city, the watchmen stand guard in vain." Psalms 127:1

My challenge for today is:

Heather's Story

On a beautiful Sunday, I picked up a notebook that was lying on the floor. Upon reading it, I realized that it was my husband's journal and that he had been having an affair with someone I knew. My shock and reaction was one of total loss of control. After a month, he owned up to the obvious of his having the affair, but also to his needing help for his sexual addiction. We both got into recovery programs…he for sex addiction, and myself for those affected by the sex addiction. We also started to see a sex addiction counselor. However, I was left with the stories I had made up about the few phrases I had read in the journal. I made up stories to try to make logic out of what was illogical. I was easily triggered back to those stories. I was told to just "get over it," that it was not happening anymore, that pretty girls are everywhere and I should not be bothered by going to places where I imagined he had been with other women. I kept being traumatized over and over again. Just when I would start to forget, a trigger would come back and the ensuing fear and pain would return.

Why could I not move forward? I decided to get therapy for myself. The counselor immediately asked if I had had disclosure. I told her no….that our couple's therapist had just told me to forget all the stories I had told myself. I told the counselor that I did not know what was true and what was not true; I was living in almost constant fear and pain even though it appeared that my spouse was sober from the addiction. Shadows of the other women were everywhere…my home, my favorite parks, my head. What had been real and what had not been real during the sixteen years when my spouse had been active in his addiction? To my surprise, my spouse agreed to do a formal disclosure. I had many questions….I had many stories needing validation. My spouse took the questions and said he wanted to answer all of them, irrespective of his counselor's advice that I be allowed to ask just a few questions. I am grateful that he said I deserved to have all of my questions answered.

The disclosure gave me clarity about many events during our marriage where I felt criticized and "not good enough." It was beneficial to me to realize that these events had nothing to do with me, but rather the negativity which had crept into our marriage due to my spouse's compulsive and frequent acting out behavior. He was truthful and told me of events which I had not even made up stories about. Although that was difficult to hear, I knew it was the truth.

When my spouse started the disclosure, he told me that this was written about behaviors of a sick person. He said that the behaviors are not the reality of him today. Listening to him, and his stopping to ask if I was okay, I realized the depth of the addiction and the pain that he had been through as well. Some of the acting out was with myself…and what I had thought was an act of love between us was not in his mind. I am coming to terms with that.

Disclosure, as difficult as acceptance of some of the events, has helped me to move past the stories in my head. I do know what is real and what is not.

Heather

My Journal

My thoughts for today:

My feelings:

What am I sensing in my body?

Can I put any meaning to my experiences?

What can I be thankful for today?

Chapter 8

Boundaries: Setting Them and Keeping Them

The goal (of boundaries) isn't to change someone else. It is to keep yourself safe and focused on healing your own wounds. (SOSA, p. 119)

Yet another trigger, new information to process; you find an old receipt from a restaurant in his pocket, your heart is racing and you can barely catch your breath. It is so difficult at the onset to trust and open yourself up again and again. It's possible that the receipt has nothing to do with his acting out behaviors. But it triggers fear, hopelessness, and the "stuck on or stuck off" pattern of activation. It seems like within seconds you can be in the "out of control," phase one — desperately seeking emotional safety. You find yourself acting out of character and doing things you never expected or thought of doing before discovery. Some of the partners have shared with me some of the desperate situations they have found themselves in, and humiliated by their actions. Behaviors they are not proud of, but knowing in their gut that something is not right. Such as bugging their spouse's phone, hacking into the acting out partner's computer, and hiring a detective. It is so painful to live in the constant thread of fear. Not feeling safe in your own skin, and feeling so out of control is paralyzing. They say sometimes it's better to look the other way.

Lindsey was aware of her husband's extra marital affairs, yet she feared the consequences of being alone, and being a single parent. She estimated that it was better to not deal with it, until her health caught up with her, and she could no longer avoid the truth.

Setting boundaries is one way of taking responsibility for yourself. It empowers your ability to stay present with your needs and limitations. Boundaries are like your personal compass. The purpose of a compass is to align ourselves in a direction that gives us a sense of reference and redirect our frame work.

The instrument is worthless if we do not adhere to it. Boundaries are for your self-protection. My first and foremost boundary is to love the Lord with all my heart, soul and mind. That requires a deep commitment and faith that He will guide me, direct me, and not give me any more than I can bear, and a way through it that enlarges a stronger empowered self. For me, this boundary not only sets a precedent, it is a way of life that demands and requires boundaries for my security against any external threats to my emotional, physical and spiritual safety.

My husband and I recently went to Las Vegas for our fortieth wedding anniversary. You might ask of all places, why there? One of my favorite secular artists was performing there, and aside from "sin city" as we were told, it also had some incredible architecture, and we were excited to experience that part of it. We were both shocked by the street advertisement, "Direct Services: girls come to you in twenty minutes." My body impulse was to snag the "girlie" cards they were handing out from their hands, both men and women involved in this incredulous act. They were targeting the men, regardless of the fact that my husband and I were walking hand in hand. I wanted to rip the cards out of their hands and fling them on the ground and say, "How does it feel to have something stolen from you, and see it scattered and broken all over the place." I did not do that but, I did say to the young man, "Do you realize how hurtful this is to relationships?" and soon realized he did not understand English. I controlled my impulse to throw more cards around in the environment, for the sake of the children all around us.

Instead of spending the next day in Las Vegas, as was planned, we booked an excursion to the Grand Canyon. That was the boundary we set. Together, for the sake of our "Sacred Space," our relationship, we switched plans. I was proud of my husband for suggesting this and the way he experienced the disgust of it all, and wanting to protect our time together, and not have it be ruined by the negative energy that was draining and felt "toxic" to us. We were able to enjoy the architecture and beauty, once removed from the "direct services."

Françoise

Boundaries, a book written more than a decade ago, by Henry Cloud, PhD, John Townsend, PhD, is a great resource to help you determine the difference between healthy and unhealthy boundaries.

The premise of this book is that you cannot control what other people say and do, but you can control how you react and make your own choices. And it explains in simple terms how to go about that. It helps put relationships into a perspective that is healthy and also nurturing. According to the authors, "Physical boundaries help us determine who may touch us and under what circumstances. Mental boundaries give us the freedom to have our own thoughts and opinions Emotional boundaries help us deal with our own emotions and disengage from the harmful, manipulative emotions of others."[11]

1. Can you identify what boundaries mean to you? How do you know when someone has violated your personal space?

| |
| |
| |
| |
| |
| |

With trauma, boundaries are generally ruptured. Traumatized people do not have the same ability as non-traumatized to discern the signals of a threat response. They are in a self-protective threat response and survival mode (fight, flight or freeze). People tend to come in and out of your personal space whether they're invited or not. Whether your boundaries are loose or rigid, your body knows when there is a violation. It tightens, constricts, and your stomach may feel jumpy along with other adverse reactions. With or without boundaries, our ability to notice our body's internal cues are

---

[11] Cloud, Henry and John Townsend. *Boundaries*, (Grand Rapids, MI: Zondervan, 1992).

often ignored. Becoming aware of your body's sense of space and what you need to feel safe can help define your boundaries and limits. These limits identify the safe and permissible people and behaviors that are allowed through your filtering system, per boundaries. There are times you may be okay in your space with people coming in and out of it. However, you need to know that if these are not safe people, and safe behaviors, you can set limits; you can decide who gets to be in there. Slow down, and allow your body's experience to resonate with what is going on.

2. Draw a stick figure of yourself in the circle on the left, and imagine there is an invisible wall between you and the other circle/person. Notice the distance you need between each other. Play around with the space; who is in there, who is not, and where are they. How much space do you need? Be curious about who you will allow in there and who you won't.

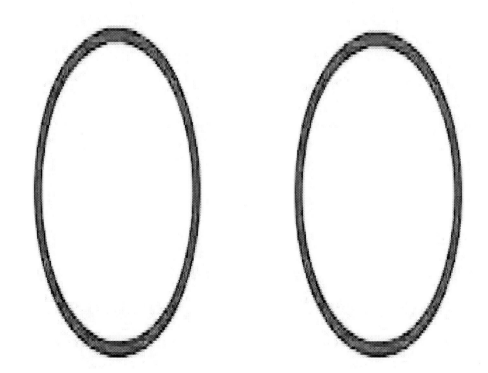

3. Notice what it's like to experience where you drew your image. Where do you need to be in your circle to feel safe, in control, and when you can just "be" in your circle? What are the conditions you need to feel safe and secure?

4. We often lose the ability to respond in our best interest when boundaries are ruptured. The sensation may feel ragged and bumpy; people are coming in and out as they choose to. In the circle on the right on the previous page, imagine an uninvited visitor making their way towards you, and notice what is going on in your body. What is it like to have an intruder coming at you?

"I keep trying to set boundaries with my husband, but he keeps breaking them, and I feel like there is no point in trying. I know I need to set limits, but whenever I do, I don't enforce them and I end up feeling more hopeless than ever." (SOSA, p. 117)

5. Can you relate to these words, and how does that resonate in your body?

A personal mission statement can be a creation of what you will and will not allow in your space. It can also be defined as your "needs list." I have seen some partners break it down to three components; physical, emotional and spiritual component,

Physically:

- I shall make time to exercise my body and experience the benefits of a strong healthy body and mind.
- I shall only allow healthy people in my space who are safe, and have boundaries for themselves.

Emotionally:

- I shall talk gently and kindly to myself, and not expect any less from anyone else.
- I shall take the time I deserve to make decisions that require any kind of limits and expectations on me.

Spiritually:

- I shall spend time in prayer and seek God's way for my life.
- I shall remove myself from the presence of evil, and not allow it to penetrate my space.

6. Mission Statements/Boundaries

Fill in the blanks. This exercise is meant to take an inventory of areas where you have violated your own principles and values, and made to feel like the "crazy one." That you are not! You have been traumatized by your spouse's sexual acting out, and your behaviors are a result of safety seeking.

"Learning to trust or re-trust your intuition as a partner to the addict is a difficult process. Family rules may have taught you to deny and minimize your feelings. The addict in your life may have led you to second-guess yourself. Addicts are good at getting spouses to deny their own reality. Part of the journey of recovery is learning to trust your own instincts." (SOSA, p.122).

7. List the ways you tend to second-guess yourself in the categories below. Be specific as to how you respond and react to yourself and others.

Trusting your thoughts and feelings:

Making decisions:

Relationships:

Healthy boundaries are flexible. Boundaries are strong enough to keep the bad stuff out and permeable enough to let the good stuff in.[12] It is the rigid and loose boundaries that are dysfunctional.

"Boundaries protect, but they shouldn't isolate you from contact with people. Removing yourself from a situation when you are unsafe is appropriate. Trusting

---

[12] Cloud & Townsend, *Boundaries.* P. 33-34.

blindly is not appropriate. Throwing yourself wide open emotionally to someone who has betrayed you is foolish. Boundaries need to be for your personal safety, not controlling the addict. Ask yourself if you are withdrawing for safety or revenge. Reconciliation and rebuilding trust is the goal," (SOSA, p.128)

There are examples of boundaries that are most common with partners of sex addicts on SOSA, page 129. List the ones below that have the most meaning to you and why. Also, be sure to list from your own experience anything that you have found helpful that may be useful to others.

1.
2.
3.
4.

5.
6.

"Addicts are notorious for using guilt trips to project responsibility for their decisions onto their spouses. Boundary crashers will convince you that if you don't do it their way, they will die and it will be your entire fault." (SOSA, p.127)

"One of the cultural traps that can hinder establishing good boundaries is giving reasons for every decision. This makes it hard to communicate clear limits." (SOSA, p.126)

8. Are they any boundary crashers in your life? How do they violate your boundaries? What makes it difficult to say no?

Boundary crashing takes a lot of energy and precious time from you. On page 132, there are examples of behaviors you may have participated in and still do. Most partners tell me they feel bad about themselves for behaving in ways they never imagined doing. For examples, Lori puts her ear to the floor above her husband's office while he is checking in with his sponsor, and Linda purchased a GPS to track her husband's where about.

9. Are there any "boundary crashing" behaviors you would like to replace with new healthy seeking behaviors. Lori still struggles with her old behavior, and now she leaves the room and goes to another part of her home where she cannot hear the conversation between her husband and his sponsor, and uses her time to meditate and journal on her healing process.

Hope for the Heart

"I am the way, and the truth, and the life. No one comes to the Father, but through me."
John 14:6

My challenge for today is:

Sherry's Story

I could not wait to marry this man that shared my dreams. Wow, how lucky am I? At the age of twenty, I was working full time while attending college waiting to be accepted into the nursing program. My parents were happily married and though they didn't agree with me marrying so young, especially before finishing school, they supported what I wanted. I had never lived anywhere but home and was very excited to start this new life with my husband.

We had spent many of our dates talking about our future, discussing financial plans, sharing religious beliefs, how soon after I finish school we would have children, how we would raise our kids, how many we would have, would I stay at home, how many vacations a year, date nights after children, buy or rent? I found myself leading most of these discussions as I had great mentors in my parents.

My fiancé would usually just agree with what I wanted and then tell me how lucky I was to have such great parents. He would then get very quiet and start to discuss his childhood. His mother had gotten pregnant in high school. His parents cheated on one another. He was beaten by his father. Every date we spent discussing our future would end in another childhood story of his. He told me when he was in Junior high his father would threaten to hang his sheets out the window if he kept wetting the bed. Every day after school he would run home so he could take the sheets in, in case his dad made good on his threat. My heart went out to him. The man I loved was hurting. I thought in my heart if I could love him enough, we could create the family he never had.

We married shortly after my birthday. It was a Friday and I arrived home from work to find a large beautifully wrapped box on the kitchen table. The instructions on the top said "open immediately." I was so excited! Inside was an outfit to wear for the evening, he even included shoes! The card said he would be home in one hour and he was taking me out; the location was a surprise.

After a lovely evening that included dinner and a play, he handed me a box. Inside was a pearl ring. I thanked, hugged and kissed him. I had had a wonderful birthday, but the dream ended quickly. As soon as we sat in the car, I could sense he was mad. In a matter of moments he was telling me how much trouble he went to pick the perfect outfit and find the best place to go. He thought I could have shown a little more excitement. The whole drive home I was so confused. What did he want? I was so thankful and happy and why was that not enough?

The next few months are somewhat a blur. He wanted us to grow as a couple, and with me working full time and going to school three nights a week, there just wasn't adequate time for us. Wanting to make him happy and our marriage as strong as possible, I quit school.

I look back to that day with great pain. The fiancé who said he supported me finishing school, was now saying everything he could to make me feel guilty about bettering myself. The next few years were filled with both of us trying to figure out marriage and his constant pressuring me to get pregnant. He was really pushing to start a family. He was going to be turning thirty and did not want to be an older father.

I had red flags about our relationship going up often but I always dismissed them. My husband just wants a family of his own and that is what I told him I wanted also. What was my problem? He always pointed out how difficult I made things; he would always take care of me and our family. I let the resentment I felt about school go and had a beautiful baby girl.

By the time she was six months old, my husband came to me and suggested I quit working. I went from full time before her birth to two nights a week after her birth. He didn't like that my focus was outside of our family. He felt work was too much, seeing as he was feeling neglected. My focus was on the baby and why couldn't I see that he needed me too. It was going to be just him and me again someday when our kids were grown, so while our daughter was young, I should be focusing on our family and keeping it strong.

I found myself doing extra things for him, making breakfast before he left for work or packing notes in his lunch so he knew I appreciated how hard he was working for our family. When he said our sex life was boring, I would try to initiate more to make him feel wanted. I was exhausted yet felt great about making my husband feel special, being a mom and still working. I continued my two nights a week until he started coming home late from work causing me to be late or forcing me to call my mother to babysit. He would always apologize, what I thought was very sincerely, and explain it was his paycheck that was providing for us. Was my "fun money" from two nights really worth the stress I was under?

I stood my ground. I loved working and being a mom. Looking back to those days, I now see the manipulation. He would be late the next few months and we would always argue the day after I worked. If I planned ahead and brought the baby to my mom, he was mad that I didn't trust he would be home like he said he would be. If I waited for him to come home so I could leave, he would be just late enough, blaming traffic or his boss talking to him after work. Always something... I gave in, I quit work. I could go back as soon as the kids were in school I told myself. It was not worth fighting with my husband. Life would now be peaceful. After all, he had what he wanted. What else could I sacrifice?

I had no idea what the next ten years of my life would hold. Around our seven year anniversary, he starting going to the gym. He thought it would be great if we could do it together. We worked out together for about four months when I noticed he would always find a reason to stay a little later at the gym. When I questioned this, he explained it took him longer than I to unwind from work.

Within a year his demeanor changed. His wardrobe was all very body revealing (tight jeans and sleeveless shirts). He started training to compete in Bodybuilding Shows. I had always lived a very healthy lifestyle that included eating "clean" and exercising. I knew his body changes were not from a healthy lifestyle. When he gave me a hug, he would squeeze me until tears fell from my eyes. When I squirmed or asked him to stop, he would snap saying other women like strong muscular men, what was my problem? When I found the steroids in his gym bag, he said he was taking them so I would be more attracted to him. He said he didn't have the time at the gym other men had because he worked such long hours to provide for us, and he wanted to get the results quicker. The little lies that I choose not to see, or justified not wanting an argument, kept coming though I was numb to them. When I found out he was cheating, it destroyed my self-esteem. I was doing everything to provide this picture perfect life. When I confronted him, it was somehow my fault because after the birth of our second child I was clearly overwhelmed by taking care of children and could not meet my husband's needs also. Of course, I was not buying this BS, yet his slow quiet voice recapping his childhood of his parent's unfaithfulness and how he never meant to hurt me actually made me feel bad for him. His tears flowed for weeks as I put my feelings aside and read tons of books on how to strengthen marriage after an affair. We went to counseling for almost three years. Of the three different counselors, each would toss around the word narcissism or co-dependence. I did not understand those terms at the time. I thought I can fix this. I can show him true love and he will change. I was wrong.

I knew who I was. Why could I not be that person now? How did I allow this man I was sharing my life with make me question what was real or not? I was in what I refer to as robot mode. Away from him I would laugh and enjoy life; with him I questioned everything including myself. If I disagreed with my husband, I never knew what I was going to get as a response, so I didn't say much. I was miserable! I think of all the days I walked on egg shells not knowing if I was getting the truth. Of the times I chose to point out what he was doing was wrong or hurtful; he always had a way of making me feel bad, guilty or responsible for his choices. I was a grown woman who knew right from wrong. I was a homemaker with two children to raise who had not completed college. I was so scared; however, I would no longer allow someone else to hijack my happiness. If not for I, then for my children, this relationship had to end. No one in my immediate family had been through divorce, or ever wanted to. This path was mine to create.

On a day I celebrate every year, I ended my twelve year marriage. We have children together so some communication is necessary; however, I altered my communication style. I have found email a great tool as he can't change my words and blame me. I plan every conversation that I know I will have with him, as it is easy to go back to that person I was when we were together if I allow myself to speak freely. I don't want or mean to go back to that place but that is what happens. When an unexpected conversation happens, I end it quickly. I constantly remind my children to stand up for themselves and what is right. I am no longer angry as I have accepted him for who he chooses to be, but instead thankful that I can finally see who he is.

    Sherry

My Journal

My thoughts for today:

My feelings:

What am I sensing in my body?

Can I put any meaning to my experiences?

What can I be thankful for today?

Chapter 9

Healing in Community

Nobody recovers by themselves. Healing will always take place in a community. (SOSA, p. 133)

My healing in part came from friends who cared and wept with me. They saw and heard my anguish, and often did not have words for me, but they stayed, and did not judge. I told my story and did not hold back on how the betrayal left me feeling lonely and scared. I researched what the impact of this could mean for me. I was not familiar with sexual addiction and didn't understand the ramifications of the damaging effects that perpetuates the cycle of rituals, tolerance levels, acting-out behaviors and disparity have on the addict and family. What I did know is that his behaviors had to stop if I was going to stay in the relationship. I needed to hold tight to my boundaries. Sometimes I felt out of control and it took the form of anger, and needed to express how hurt I was that he could keep a secret from me for so many years. My anger had its purpose; it kept me from minimizing, rationalizing any of his behaviors, and doing what I knew to be safety seeking. I insisted he install Covenant Eyes on the computer, an Internet accountability program. I knew I wasn't crazy, and his addiction was not going to make me feel that way. I was experiencing the betrayal of the couple trauma and needed my support system for validation and support.

Group settings for partners can be re-traumatizing when you hear words such as, "You're a co-addict, addicted to the addict." Partners have been wounded with words like, "lose some weight, have more sex, don't you know you're chasing him away? "This may come from friends, family and unfortunately, therapists as well. Even though Liz shudders at the word co-addict, which is regularly used in her group, she has developed relationships and has the support she needs from her local S-Anon group. Find the safe people; attend a group that supports what you are experiencing.

As a trauma model group facilitator, Hope for the Heart, I enjoy watching women grow at their pace, wherever they are in the process of healing from the wounds of betrayal, and having their feelings validated by one another is so encouraging to me. They are awesome women that have faced the courage to process their trauma and deal with the difficult changes that had to transpire for mobility and movement towards healing.

My community helped me find my voice and trust my thoughts, feelings, and actions without wavering. I am stronger and unwavering because of their support, and because I trusted in a God who gives me inner strength and courage, I too, can be there for other women who struggle with betrayal.

Françoise

"Nobody recovers in isolation! Every spouse must have a group or they won't survive. These friendships will be the source of healing." (SOSA, p.123)

Not all support groups are the same. It's important that you do your research and take the time to develop relationships in the safest possible environment for your journey. Your network of friends and confidants is sacred. Hold it as a precious gift close to your heart. These are the people who will walk with you through the dark days of your journey and will celebrate the victories with you.

When early mental health and addiction specialists began to recognize the problem of compulsive and destructive sexual behavior in people's lives, they naturally turned to the model that had provided the only broadly helpful road map for society's other destructive habits: the addiction model. From that model, they coined the term "sex addict." However, the 12–step sex addiction model takes it one step further. Not only are partners of sex addicts affected, those partners are also addicted. They are addicted to the sex addict.[13]

Partners receive the label of "co-addict" automatically, simply because they love the sex addict. It does not matter that many partners knew nothing of the person's addiction prior to making a commitment. Nor does it matter that the partner may not have seen recognizable signs of the addiction's existence. The theory holds that partners develop co-addicted traits and characteristics over time due to the fact that they are in relationships with addicts.[14]

"Two are better than one, because they have a good return for their labor: If either of them falls down, one can help the other up. But pity anyone who falls and has no one to help them up." Ecclesiastes 4:9-10

You may feel lonely and hopeless at the onset of discovery. Not everyone understands sexual addiction. Jennie's husband had a dual diagnosis; he was an alcoholic and a sex addict. When he went for treatment of his sex addiction, she had a harder time telling people he was in treatment for sex addiction than she did when he went in for his substance abuse. She thought people would judge her and that somehow this was her fault; not enough sex with her husband, not pretty enough, and not smart

---

[13] Steffens and Means.. 24.
[14] Ibid. 25.

enough. It was a lonely journey and when Jennie finally found a support group for spouses of sex addicts, she was told to "stay on her side of the street" when she experienced any threat of her spouse's acting out. Her safety-seeking behavior was called "controlling," and she was labeled a "co-addict,"[15] addicted to the addict.

1. Has this been the case for you? How have you experienced this?

| |
| |
| |
| |
| |

Ann writes, "Why should I go to a group? He's the one with the problem. I don't need any more public humiliation. If he can fix his problem things will be ok. I tried listening to other people's stories but it was too depressing. It makes me angry all over again." (SOSA, p.133)

2. Can you relate to Ann's story? If so, what has that been like for you?

If this is not the case, can you state how different it's been for you to be a part of a community that supports you?

| |
| |
| |
| |
| |

---

[15] Richard Blankenship, Barbara Steffens, and Marsha Means address the problems connected with the concept of "co-addiction."

Sharing your story can be frightening and risky at first. But it can also be a healing experience with safe people. Partners of sex addicts often fear rejection and shame if the secret is told. Perhaps you have found yourself defending the addict, trying to keep extended family members from finding out, trying to keep from involving an employer, etc. Keeping secrets is harmful. I am not suggesting that you need to tell everyone you know. But that you have a safe support system in place that empathizes and validates where you are and your healing process.

For months, Jennie's family had no idea that her husband had been in treatment for sexual addiction. They thought he was being treated for alcohol addiction. Can you imagine how difficult it would be to hold onto that kind of information when you are hurting so deeply, and you have no one to tell?

3. Does Jennie's story resonate with you? If so, can you take a step toward your healing process and write about what it's been like to hold onto the painful secrets.

You are not the one who has to be the "truth teller" for the addiction. But it is important to be aware of how the addiction has impacted you and is still impacting your body, mind and spirit. It is up to you, who and what you choose to tell is your decision.

4. What are some qualities in a person that you can trust as a safe person you could talk to?

5. How do you know that they are someone you can trust?

"It has been rare that I have ever seen a spouse regret joining a therapy group. The only complaint I ever get on our groups is that the spouses hate to see them end. The spouses build friendships that begin to meet their needs. I've watched them develop friendships that have a level of depth that people deeply desire. Issues of trust, intimacy and boundaries can heal in groups." (SOSA, p.140).

6. What are some steps/boundaries you might take towards trusting someone with your story?

7. What is it like to think you could give yourself permission to put aside any blame, shame or humiliation, and choose to be a truth teller with those whom you trust?

8. What are some of the benefits of support networking? (SOSA, p.135-144)

9. What are some of the challenges you may encounter in building a support network? (SOSA, p.135 -144)

A safe and supportive community can be a gift to you and part of your journey that keeps you from the shame and isolation. The words, "me too" are comforting coming from a group member who knows and understands your pain. Knowing you aren't alone is helpful for your healing journey.

As a partner of a sex addict, you need support, validation and accountability; such as what takes place in a support group, and with people you can learn to trust and experience safety. With each other's help and sharing experiences, you can develop new behaviors and ways of coping with the trauma. Some of the common areas where partners struggle are emotional dishonesty (saying things are okay when they are not); stuffing feelings and pretending they aren't real; and developing destructive coping mechanisms that are destructive for your health and healing.

10. How can people in a support group provide the help you need and make a difference for you?

| |
| |
| |
| |
| |
| |
| |

11. If you are in a support group, or have been, what resources have been there for you?

| |
| |
| |
| |
| |

"I victimized myself many times by wanting to be in the giving role constantly, and not being able to receive. Irrational giving, spending, and other forms of one-way intimacy led ultimately to feelings of resentment and frustration. It was the support and accountability found in a group that helped me to overcome these patterns. It was also a safe place to learn to receive" (SOSA, p.139).

12. Are there any fears you may have or experiences that keep you from joining/participating in a group?

13. Read about the different types of groups. (SOSA, p. 142-143) Have you experienced any of these groups? What was the group like for you? How was the group helpful?

14. Is there anything that could have made the group a safer place for you?

Hope for the Heart

"Behold, I stand at the door and knock; if anyone hears My voice and opens the door,
I will come in to him and will dine with him, and he with Me."
Revelations 3:20

My challenge for today is:

Allysa's Story

My father was a sex addict and alcoholic, and my mother was molested by her father. I grew up with two emotionally distant parents, and I didn't understand how to set boundaries and form healthy, supportive relationships with friends and family. All I knew was I wanted to do better than my family, but I didn't have the tools necessary to do this.

When I started dating my ex, he was sweet and attentive, but that didn't last long. At first, he couldn't do enough for me. I felt like he was really safe, that he was someone who would always take care of me and never cheat on me. He seemed to be thrilled that I would return his feelings. After we got married, I suddenly became invisible to him. He didn't talk to me, didn't ask my thoughts or opinions or even what I had been up to during the day. He would reject me when I initiated sex, and he would initiate sex only in the middle of the night after I was sound asleep.

After less than a year of marriage, the discoveries started and continued every few years for the next twenty-one years. Porn, a pair of women's underwear, condoms, a Valentine not for me, etc. He made excuses and accused me of overreacting. I was confused about whether to believe his explanations and afraid of what would happen to me and my children if I left. We had moved every few years for medical school, residency, fellowship, and finally joining a medical practice, so I didn't have much of a support system. My family was thousands of miles away. We were in marriage counseling with various therapists over the years, and they all seemed to accept his explanations without question, so I felt like I really must be overreacting.

Finally, after fifteen years, he was identified as a sex addict. He started a 12- Step Program. We went to more marriage counseling, and things got worse. The therapist told him that he needed to be more assertive and that no one could deny his reality. As a result, he would not back down from his cognitive distortions. It seemed every move I made or comment I uttered could somehow be twisted to show I was trying to hurt him or that I was to blame for a problem.

For example, one time the therapist assigned us reading. The book explained the difference between complaints and criticisms. A complaint is about a specific thing someone does; a criticism attacks someone's character. One day I had a complaint. He had stayed home to take care of our son while I was sick, except he left our son with me and disappeared for hours. I tried calling for him, but he didn't answer. I asked my son to find Daddy, but he couldn't find him. Finally, around lunchtime, my ex popped into the bedroom. Remembering the lesson from the book, I said, "I feel disappointed that you left our son in here all morning when I asked you to stay home and take care of him." His reaction was shocking. He yelled at me in front of our son for criticizing him, telling me that nothing he did ever made me happy, I could never be happy, he didn't deserve to be treated like this, etc. I grabbed the book and showed him how I had used the exact wording for a complaint, not a criticism. His reply? "The book is wrong! Anyone in the world could see that the book is wrong!" I apologized for upsetting him, telling him that I didn't intend to hurt him. He yelled back at me that I had to admit that I criticized him intentionally or he would not accept my apology. How could I admit to something I didn't do? He continued to yell at me off and on for three days, even after I crawled up the stairs to our guest room and locked the door, begging him to leave me alone.

Whenever I tried to set a boundary, he would escalate the stakes so that he knew I would back down. He said he was just setting his own boundaries with consequences.

It's not just the sexual acting out that was painful. He has willing to hurt me—to lie, blame, gaslight, etc.—in all aspects of our relationship. Too often I took his bait and tried to defend myself or reason with him when I should have just not responded.

Luckily, throughout the years of marriage counseling, I worked really hard on myself and my other relationships. I learned how to establish healthy boundaries with my friends and family and to reach out to people who were good for me. When I finally discovered that he had been having group sex and going to prostitutes, I had developed the tools and support system that I needed to finally set a boundary and throw him out. He had no interest in seeking the kind of treatment I thought he needed, so I filed for divorce. Because of the hard work I did in therapy, I am learning that I can trust my own instincts and can rely on the support of my friends and family.

The most valuable things I have learned being married to a sex addict is to attend to your own needs to keep yourself strong. Trust your gut. Be very careful about marriage counseling— traditional marriage counseling won't work unless both partners have done their own work. Most marriage counselors do not understand SA. Find your own therapist who can help you grow regardless of what happens in the marriage. Make sure they understand the trauma of being married to an SA. Do not let anyone call you a co-addict. The shame and humiliation is his, not yours. Get support—tell your trusted friends and family or find a support group that will help meet your needs. It's tough to make decisions with your head, when your heart is hurting so badly. A supportive community can help you keep your head on straight while supporting you emotionally. You don't have to be alone in this experience.

This is not about you, this is not about you, this is not about you!

Allysa

My Journal

My thoughts for today:

My feelings:

What am I sensing in my body?

Can I put any meaning to my experiences?

What can I be thankful for today?

Chapter 10

Your Grief Will Turn to Joy: The Forecast

Each person's journey is unique. (SOSA, p. 145)

Have hope dear one, I understand your pain, and yet I want you to know that some of the women I work with have similar stories and they have found hope and healing and the courage to go on. Similar stories, but also very unique. It's important that you share your story. There is healing in journaling and telling and hearing yourself say it out loud. There is validation in knowing that someone else feels and hears where you're coming from. You are heard and not judged; you are cared for and not criticized. Wherever you are in your journey, give yourself credit for making it this far. You are reading and working this book, you got up this morning, if you have children, you fed them; got them off to school; went to work; put yourself together; something that at this time of your life may not be easy. Today is a new day, and where it starts and end is not so important as how you are doing, and what you are doing about it. If the addiction is fairly new information for you, you are where many of us were from the very beginning of this journey. I remember Ella saying to me "My husband's addiction has changed me, and for the good."

Even if it's been months and years, as it's been for Carla, without a formal disclosure, her husband continues to have slips, and she goes into "freeze," feeling helpless. *Spouses of Sex Addicts, Hope for the journey,* and this workbook are one of many tools that can help you along this difficult place. You must take time to take care of yourself, and not be in any hurry to rush into anything or any decision. If you know in your heart, the wounds of this addiction are beyond getting to a place of healing and restoration with your husband, and you have to get to the "light at the end of the tunnel" on your own, that is between you and God. Seek help from professionals and clergy you trust that can give you wise counsel. Do not hold onto any guilt that is not your own. Don't allow anyone else's story of success that differs from yours to fill you with shame. Your success is about making it through today, sometimes it's moment by moment, finding the courage within yourself to be authentic and maintain your boundaries and needs.

As time went on, I knew my grief was not as intense when the frequency and duration of triggers did not have the same compelling drive to draw me into a helpless and hopeless place. It took time to trust with my heart, head and eyes. Trust your process and know that you cannot hurry through your grief. To get to the "thankful" part of the grief is knowing that the process of experiencing the grief has made you stronger, and believe me and many others, you will be thankful for that.

Françoise

"Spouses don't always end up in the same place. I have found that when both an addict and spouse make the decision to do individual and couples recovery that the marriages not only survive, they thrive. The reality is that not all marriages will survive." (SOSA, p.145).

Read the stories in SOSA, Chapter 10 (Marianne, Jill, Melvin, and Janet). Not every detail will apply to you; however, the pain of betrayal will resonate and have its own personal meaning. Remember to slow yourself down if the stories bring up anxiety and difficult emotions. Take time out to do some self-care. Notice where in your body you feel solid and grounded. Focus on this as well as staying present with the hard stuff. It's not easy to hold the difficult stuff and be present, it takes practice. Move back and forth between both the difficult and the pleasant, the grounding experience of being in the here and now. Think of the color "blue" as the grounding, pleasant place to want to be in, and where there is blue, there is a red, as in the triggers and hard place to be. It does not mean that the "red' has to take you over to the "on or off" place. However, noticing it and working it can bring a sense of cohesiveness back into your body.

So, we really want to stretch the blue, pleasant place, be with it and hang out with it as long as you are able. Life ebbing and flowing. When you are in a red zone, slow yourself down, breath! Get to know when your broaching the intensity of what your body is experiencing. It may feel like a gut wrenching pain in your chest. Be aware of it, and notice if there is any meaning to the experience. When you are ready to return to the assignment, notice what it was like for you to have taken the time to honor what came up for you.

1. What did you notice, and what was that like? What meaning did you assign to the experience?

| |
| |
| |
| |

The people in these stories are real. Their coping strategies helped them to manage their trauma and betrayal. Whether right or wrong, it's what they hung onto to get through some difficult times. Your story is what it is, regardless of some similarities. Everyone learns to manage pain with or without help, support, and tools. We all have to do the best we could under traumatic circumstances. With God's help, Marianne had the courage to say, "Now that I have begun my journey with a group of supportive and wonderful ladies, I wouldn't trade it for anything. God continued to reveal Himself to me in ways that have been healing the hurts of the past. I'm grateful that I can share my story and that I have a voice."

God began a good work in Marianne, and He never left her side. In the fourth hour, as the disciples faced the wind, they were battered and frightened by it. "But Jesus immediately said to them: "Take courage! It is I. Don't be afraid." Matthew 14:27

2. Each of these people chose to be vulnerable and open their hearts. They had a desire to come along side and encourage the reader through their pain and how they got through it. As you read about Marianne, what parts of her story connect with you?

3. How do Marianne's words on page 149 (SOSA) resonate with you, "Now I know the greatest tragedy in my life would be to *not find myself.*" Express what that might be like for you.

| |
| |
| |
| |
| |
| |

4. Marianne experienced spiritual abuse from her pastor after seeking spiritual guidance and support. Has spiritual abuse been part of your journey? How do you think you would have responded to spiritual abuse?

| |
| |
| |
| |
| |
| |

Jill also suffered spiritual abuse. "I knew that as a Christian wife, it was my duty to forgive, to trust, to understand and to pray for my husband. I did not know what to do with my feelings of fear and bitterness, but I believed those feelings were wrong and whatever problems I had in loving my husband were my problem." (SOSA, p.150)

Trauma repetition is characterized by repeated self-destructive behaviors that may have had their origin in childhood. It is unfinished business that is driven subconsciously to relive/re-make the story. A re-enactment of the past and repeating painful experiences in the present that is reminiscent of previous trauma in your life.

For example, Lucy finds herself in repeated physically abusive relationships. As a child, she witnessed her mother getting "beat up" repeatedly by boyfriends.

5. Can you think of anything in your life that may look like trauma repetition, something from the past that seemingly is being reenacted in the present?

| |
| |
| |
| |
| |
| |

If you can relate to the previous question, you may want to look into seeking a therapist who is equipped to address any patterns/behaviors from the past that have influenced the present, someone who is trained to work with trauma victims.

Eye Movement Desensitizing and Reprocessing (EMDR) is a successful intervention that enables you to access positive ways of reframing the original trauma (reprocessing). You can find a therapist for this specialty in your area by accessing,

http://www.emdr.com/francine-shapiro-phd.html.

Somatic Experience (SE) is another successful modality that promotes healing from the past injuries, and in the frame work of how the body holds the trauma. You can find a therapist in your area that practices this healing process by accessing,

http://www.traumahealing.com/somatic-experiencing/index.html.

Chapter 2, *Spouses of Addicts*, describes various forms of trauma treatment.

Jill had a moment of clarity that changed her life forever. "Something happened that flipped a switch in my brain. I did not want the rest of my life to look like this." (SOSA P. 150)

6. Has there been a "moment" like this for you? It does not need to be a huge "flip of a switch." It can be as simple as today you went to a meeting, and were able to say, "Someone validated my feelings, changed my life forever. "What was it?

7. What has that moment like for you? How has it changed you?

Melvin is the male spouse of a female sex addict. Sex addiction in women may be more common than previously believed. Here are a few frightening statistics on Women with Pornography Addiction:

- 30% of those admitting to sexual addiction are women.[16]
- 34% of women in one poll admitted to using Internet pornography and one out of every six women reported struggles with addiction to pornography."[17] This is an increase from a survey in the 1970s in which less than 10% of Christian women admitted to viewing pornography.

"I attended a workshop for spouses in Atlanta. There were only two male spouses including myself, but the group quickly accepted us after getting over the initial shock of seeing men in the room." (SOSA, p.153)

8. Does Melvin's story and statistics surprise you? Why or why not?

"At the workshop, the other man who was there was about 7 years into his journey of recovery with his wife. He told me it took him about 2 years to get over all the search, seizure and spying activities. I am beginning to have more good days than bad days. I don't get as depressed as I used to, and I now know it isn't my fault that my wife made the choices she did." (SOSA, p.154)

---

[16] Internet-filter-review.com
[17] Lacy, Janie, *Today's Christian Woman*, May 24, 2010.

9. How do you think Melvin got to be at a place in his life where he could say, "I know it isn't my fault?"

Janet's story states that her husband's behaviors triggered her "deep fear of abandonment."

10. Can you relate to her feelings? And why?

11. What are some things you have done in your moments of disparity? Leave any shame out of this and stay with your new reality as safety- seeking behaviors.

| |
| |
| |
| |
| |
| |

Editor's note: Janet identifies herself as a co-addict. She was able to use a 12-step tradition (take what works and throw away the rest) and had a successful journey with S-Anon.

"But slowly I started to get it. His disease was not about me. I did not cause it. I could not control it. All I could control was me. God was revealing Himself to me; sometimes daily. I was broken. He started to rebuild me. He would lead me to places in His word where I could find hope. He would lead me to places that would comfort me. I found my desire for Him start to increase. I was reading about how we had to go through trials to perfect our faith. I read that God sets prisoners free through trials.

I am exactly where I am meant to be. Jesus set me free by causing me to walk through the fire. I still feel hurt. I still have a deep wound inside. There are days when I cannot believe what pain I have walked and am still walking through. But I can tell you that Jesus never left my side. I believe he allowed this to happen so that my life purpose might be fulfilled and so that His will may be done." (SOSA, p.157, 158).

Janet slowly got that her husband's addiction was not about her. Is there any part of your spouse's acting out behaviors that you find yourself rationalizing and minimizing? For example, on multiple occasions, Lisa would walk in a room and find her husband viewing pornography, she denied the addiction by telling herself that "It's a man thing.

All men do this, at least he's home with me and he's not physically with another woman."

12. Can you be willing to share this with your group/friend and receive some helpful and caring suggestions that may help you to see a different perspective?

| |
| |
| |
| |
| |
| |

13. Janet was able to say "I am exactly where I am meant to be?" This may or may not be your experience? Remember your story. Where you are right now is where you need to be. We process one step at a time. Can you be okay with that? Why or why not?

| |
| |
| |
| |
| |
| |

Notice what is going on for you and use your "personal journal" to document it.

Hope for the Heart

"He fulfills the desires of those who fear him; he hears their cry and saves them." Psalms 145:19

My challenge for today is:

Chris and Laura's Story

"One of the fears I had when Laura found out was having to tell her everything. I was afraid she would leave me. I didn't want to keep secrets. I was scared to hold on and scared to let go. I didn't want to hurt her anymore—I just didn't know what to do. Then we go into a counselor's office and she starts talking about disclosure. I feared the worst. Laura would want to know all of the details and we would never get over it. My stomach sank and I felt like I couldn't breathe." (Chris)

"I just needed the truth. It felt like I was crazy. I wanted to feel sane. There was nothing I could count on—he had lied so much. I feared the worst. The truth would hurt, yet the nightmares hurt worse. I didn't think I could take anymore. I couldn't sleep through the night. I would have a nightmare and then wake up with my mind stuck in a state of fear. What had he done that I don't know about? The things I know about are horrible. What if it's worse? I felt like my brain was going to explode. I needed to know the truth.

The counselor said she would guide us through the process of disclosure. We were scared, yet felt relief at the same time. She didn't try to sugar coat it. It would be difficult, but she would be there to advocate for me.

Chris wrote a letter detailing what he had done. The counselor gave him a copy of the chapter on disclosure from the Spouses of Sex Addicts *book. They worked on the letter and then came the day. I had told the women in my group that I might need to call them after the disclosure. I was grateful that they were there for me. Our counselor guided us through the session. She gave me the freedom to take a break if I needed it. I asked questions and definitely let him know how hurt I was. I was shocked, hurt, and angry. I was glad we drove separate cars. I couldn't stand for him to go home to the same house. He stayed with his parents that night.*

It's now been almost two years since that day. Eventually, finding out the truth gave me a strange sense of relief. I guess I could deal with what I knew to be true. He even asked if he could take a polygraph afterwards. I hadn't even thought of having him take one. He passed. It hurt to go through it, yet it would have hurt more to live with the fear. I still have the feelings and memories come back at times. There are still some sleepless nights. We don't keep secrets anymore. As tough as it was, our marriage would have been stuck forever if we hadn't gone through disclosure. In some ways, it was like cutting open an infected boil. It hurt and it was messy, yet it was the beginning of healing. There are still days I'd like to push him off of a bridge, but not as much as I did when I first found out. We now share things in our relationship that had never been shared before. I was scared, frightened, and reluctant. As I look back, I know now that we had to go through what I call the emotional surgery—and there wasn't any anesthesia. I'm glad I did it, and I'm glad it's over!" (Laura)

Chris and Laura

My Journal

My thoughts for today:

My feelings:

What am I sensing in my body?

Can I put any meaning to my experiences?

What can I be thankful for today?

Chapter 11

Redeeming the Pain: Hope for the Journey

Although our relationship is in the process of being restored and redeemed with God's grace and goodness, there continues to be valleys that we must walk through. (SOSA, p. 159)

My greatest resource has been my relationship with God. In the depths of my disparity, I found hope in knowing that God heard my voice, and that "I am fearfully and wonderfully made," Psalms 139:14. In his image…there are no mistakes with Him.

"No temptation has overtaken you except what is common to mankind. And God is faithful; he will not let you be tempted beyond what you can bear. But when you are tempted, he will also provide a way out so that you can endure it." 1 Corinthians 10:13

I have endured and God has been faithful to hold me in the palm of His hand. He is my foundation and spiritual rock. In my search for God's ways and healing, He taught me that there were things about myself that I needed to surrender to Him. I searched to seek and understand His will through scripture and love Him above all things, places, and people. He "enlarged my heart." I now have a greater capacity to forgive, to understand, love, and I have empathy for those who hurt like I did when I initially found out about my husband's secret. My heart rejoices for the many blessings in my life. I now can share my story and give hope and help to other men and women who have been impacted by sexual addiction.

I love the book of Psalms in the Old Testament. David is a man after God's own heart and yet, David sinned detestably against His God. He lusted after another man's wife, and after finding out she was pregnant with his child, he had Bathsheba's husband put in the front lines of duty knowing he would be killed. David had the authority to do this, and he did, but it caused a tremendous amount of pain to all involved, especially the heart of God. David cries out in his despair and shame, and in the end he is restored.

"I run in the path of your commands, for you have broadened my under-standing." Psalms 119:32

Initially, working with the partners was triggering for me, as I heard them tell their stories and their experiences I could not help but resonate with parts of it. My heart would go out to them and be triggered and later fall apart, and be angry at my husband that I was put in this position. The energy that I was pouring into my clients was the redeeming grace for my journey; I was able to give to them what I also needed for myself. Hope from a God that has compassion for the hurting. Now when I hear the stories, I have a new appreciation and hope to give because the pain that broke me is the pain that made me who I am today. I am much stronger in my ability to face the hard stuff, and my faith has been strengthened by a God who has never left me, I take courage and look to the future as a refuge.

I still tear up at times when I hear stories, but my prayer is that the Lord will give me the exact thoughts and words they need to hear in that moment. I am inspired by their courage to face their wounds and feelings toward the addict and themselves, and how they become stronger by processing their deepest hurts.

Can you make it your hope and prayer to have God "enlarge your heart" through this difficult journey?

Françoise

"There was a distance between my husband and me. There was a lack of emotional intimacy and connection. There were certainly good moments and pleasant events, but the more I looked to him to be my soul-mate and meet my emotional needs, the more separated we became. When he was happy and content, then I could be relaxed and peaceful. Once I had that formula figured out, I worked my life around makings things go easily and peacefully. I was OK! My value, emotions, and meaning of life were all centered on his response to me." (SOSA, p.160).

1. Debbie went through much of what spouses typically experience. Comparisons, feelings of inadequacy, and attempts to manage her husband's struggle. Do you relate to any part of Debbie's story? What might that be?

In time, Debbie was able to prioritize her relationships in the "correct order:" God first, and secondly, her husband.

2. What does "correct order" mean and look like to you?

It may be that you are just now hearing about a loving God who desires to be in fellowship with you; who wants to help you through this difficult time. If you are willing to confess with your mouth that Jesus is Lord, and died to save you from your sins, you too, can be in a relationship that changes your life and hope for the future.

"He told me it was a CD that had come from a friend. I threatened to call that boy's mother. Everyone should know about this, I thought. Then my son said it was really his daddy's pornography. I was shocked, angry and scared." (SOSA, p.161)

"Christian sisters in the group challenged me to be honest, transparent and authentic with my feelings, which were extremely difficult. After all, the facade that all was well had been my coping mechanism for most of my life." (SOSA, p. 164)

Developing an emotional vocabulary is an important part of your journey. They are your feelings. Own them, be with them, and don't dismiss them. As you practice being with your feelings, you may notice you are able to tolerate and deactivate the activation. Notice if there are any sensations, images, thoughts, and meaning that may be associated with what's going on.

3. Debbie stated that she put on a "façade that all is well." This had been her coping mechanism. Is this something that resonates with you? Draw a picture of what it feels like when you pretend that everything is okay but you know in your heart it's not.

"Today, I continue to learn to recognize, admit and explore my feelings. Sometimes the pendulum swings too far from the center in my attempt to discover and explore how I really feel. But I have discovered great freedom and peace as I am becoming more skilled with transparency and authenticity in my emotions." (SOSA, p.166)

This next assignment is meant to give you an awareness and history of where some of your emotions may originate. John Gottman is a renowned researcher in the areas of relationships and emotions. Take your time, this is a helpful instrument, but may bring "stuff" up, slow down and breathe , and you will get through it with less activation.

The History and Philosophy of your Emotions

(From The Gottman Institute, Inc. Training Manual)[18]
Used with permission

A. Anger

What is the history of your experience with the emotion of anger? Could you tell if your parents were angry? What was this experience like for you? Could your parents tell if you were angry? How did they react to your anger? What was it like in your family growing up?

---

[18] Copyright 2000-2009 by Dr. John M Gottman and Dr. Julie Schwartz Gottman, Distributed under license by The Gottman Institute, Inc. (17-131.)

B. Sadness:

What is the history of your experience with the emotion of sadness? Could you tell if your parents were sad? What was this experience like for you? Could your parents tell if you were sad? How did they react to your sadness? What was it like in your family growing up?

C. Fear:

What is the history of your experience with the emotion of fear? How did your family respond when you felt insecure? Could you tell if your parents were afraid? What was this experience like for you? Could your parents tell if you were afraid or worried? How did they react to your fears? How do you deal with another's worries and fears in this marriage or partnership? What was it like in your family growing up?

D. Love:

What is the history of your experience with the emotion of love? How did your parents show you that they loved you? Was your family growing up very affectionate? What was this experience like for you? Could your parents tell if you need affection? How did they react to your need for affection and love? How do you show that you love each other in this relationship? What was it like in your family growing up?

E. Pride:

What is the history of your experience with the emotion of pride? How did your parents shoe you that they were proud of you? Could you tell if your parents were proud of your accomplishments? What was this experience like for you? Could your parents tell if you wanted them to be proud of you? How did you react to your achievements and triumphs? How does your partner express pride in you? Do you express pride in your partner? What was it like in your family growing up?

F. Your philosophy about expressing negative emotions:

What is your philosophy about expressing emotions? What was it like in your family growing up? Are there differences between you and your spouse in the expression and experience of emotion? What role do these differences play in your relationship?[19]

[19] Copyright © 2000-2009 by Dr. John Gottman and Dr. Julie Schwartz Gottman. Distributed under license by the Gottman Institute Inc. Used with permission from The Gottman Institute, Inc.

4. What was the hardest part of this exercise for you?

5. Draw pictures of yourself with the emotions you felt with each feeling during the exercise, and where in your body you felt the sensation of the emotion. Use colored pencils to indicate each emotion and its intensity.

"When my husband returns to the home, there will be further boundaries in place to protect me. While he is not in the home, I have been safe. When he returns, we will live as roommates, in separate rooms of the house. He will do his own laundry, prepare his own meals, and court me before I will be able to fully have a marriage relationship with him." (SOSA, p.167)

"My pain has had a purpose. Today I am blessed to be a part of a fellowship of spouses on an incredible journey. We share our victories and our pain. I have relationships that would have never existed otherwise. I've learned that God has a purpose for me as I've struggled to make sense of things. I don't always understand why things happen, but I see God's hand in each struggle." (SOSA, p.169)

6. Is there anything about Debbie's boundaries that you might be curious about, why or why not?

Debbie's story is one of redemption. She works with spouses' groups and has shared her story all over the country. It was critical that she do her own work first. God didn't waste her pain. Your journey may or may not involve leading a group, or sharing your story publicly, but God will work in your life to help you redeem the pain.

Having boundaries is an important part of a healthy lifestyle. Managing slips was a part of Debbie's story. What are your thoughts about Debbie "putting boundaries in place to protect me?"

Hope for the Heart

"I will repay you for the years the locusts have eaten—the great locust and the young locust, the other locusts and the locust swarm—my great army that I sent among you." Joel 2:25

My challenge for today is:

Debbie's Story (Updated)

It's been five years since I wrote my story for the book S.A.R.A.H. *The release of a workbook makes it a great time for an update. During those years, there have been many reality checks. They serve as dark reminders of the addiction and the many areas of life it permeates. This is also a time to reflect on growth and healing. During the first years I just wanted to get through this alive. When you are grieving and feeling the enormous pain, you just try to survive. At times the comments people would make felt like a knife going through me. I felt isolated, lonely and devastated. When you hurt so badly, you just want life to stop. Why couldn't life have a "pause" button that I could push? Let me grieve, get things together, and then push the "start" button again. That's how it felt, but reality is different. I did keep busy. Sometimes in ways that were healthy and others were probably a way to avoid pain. One of the great joys has been leading a spouse's support group. This community of ladies has been phenomenal. Their support can't be measured. It is priceless. This is not a journey to take by yourself. Isolation breeds shame and resentment, both of which are toxic. Community provides support and safety as you face the realities of life with a sex addict.*

I've seen the impact on my grown children as they face the challenges of marriage, family, and life in general. Children learn about marriage from their parents. At times it has scared the living poo right out of me. During these five years we have become grandparents. This has been joyful and I wouldn't trade it for the world. It's also a reality check as I think about what their lives will be like. Nothing makes you face reality like seeing your children live out the things they have learned from their parents. This has been wonderful a t times, and scary at others.

In reflecting on the last five years, I can say that my grace bucket is extremely low. Through all of the healing that has taken place, there is still the reality that this could happen again. I expect honesty, and won't tolerate anything less. I know I won't stand for this crap again. My husband has demonstrated that he wants to be honest with me. We live one day at a time. Honesty is a foundational standard of our marriage. I don't expect perfection. I do expect faithfulness.

Recovery has led to some amazingly deep conversations, and I know that there are more that are needed. Marriage is a journey, whether you are married to a sex addict or not. I've learned that I can control how I react, regardless of what others choose to do.

God has been faithful. At times, it can feel like you have been led out into the wilderness to suffer and die. Life has gone on. At times it has been painful, and at others it has brought joy beyond measure. Take your journey of healing and share your story with others. It's one of the most healing things you can do for yourself and for others.

Debbie

My Journal

My thoughts for today:

My feelings:

What am I sensing in my body?

Can I put any meaning to my experiences?

What can I be thankful for today?

Chapter 12

Pearls of Wisdom:
Learning from the Voice of Experience

*The spouses who have shared their journey have
given us great pearls of wisdom. (SOSA, p. 172)*

As part of my story I have chosen to write the workbook for Spouses of Sex Addicts: Hope for the Journey. I never expected to do anything like this and I have been so blessed. I never imagined working with a population of women who suffered from the trauma of sexual betrayal in their relationships.

My story is not over yet, I trusted that God had plans to use me in this capacity and He has not failed me. One of the blessings for me personally, has been to experience God turn "my mourning into joy." I have seen the women move forward in a direction that is healing and best suited for them. Their strength and courage has excited and validated exactly where I need to be and given me meaning to fulfill God's purpose in my life through in this journey.

The progress comes in small bits and pieces. Experiencing the moments of clarity and connection with the women I work with and they are able to look at me and say, "That makes sense, I get it, I have some relief, I feel heard, I am seeing the bigger picture, and this was so helpful." She has done the hard work of expanding her awareness and capacity to have a greater internal strength to get through the best she possibly can.

I spoke with Bella this morning. She sounded strong as she told me that she had filled for a divorce. The last thing in the world she wanted was another divorce. Now she faces having to sell her home, find an apartment that is suitable for her children, and yet, she is peaceful. "My children and I have not experienced this in a long time, and we are so much better because of it." Bella was the quiet one in the relationship, and would acquiesce to her husband's wants and needs, regardless of it being right or wrong. It was her duty and life mission to make him happy, even at her own expense. This often left her feeling like she didn't matter. Her inner wisdom told her that he was being unfaithful, and lying to her about his recovery. Group helped her to find her inner voice; she had a lot at risks, but willing to do what she needed to do to get clarity and mental health. "Whatever it takes I will do it for my kids. We'll live in a two bedroom apartment if need be." It initially took her children to motivate her to do something so different and out of her realm of comfort. She found her inner courage and was able to face the fears she had of being alone. Her authenticity showed up in her principles and values as she stayed true to her inner voice. Soon after her husband moved out, Bella heard that he had another girlfriend.

A friend of mine said, "You will get as far with your clients as you are willing to go yourself." My prayer to God was, "I am willing to do whatever you want me to do; show me what you want; direct me, open doors, close doors," and the only way I know to be in His will and experience that level of attunement with Him is to be in His word. My greatest sense of stability is the maker of all of what I am and who I am.

I wanted to be a resource and means of using my pain in helping women get through their toughest times and offer the support they needed. I wanted women to know that in most cases, this addiction existed long before the relationship with their spouses.

You are not to blame, and what you are feeling and experiencing is real, honor yourself; your needs, thoughts, and feelings. Please do not dismiss yourself. You are worth the time it takes to experience the peace, as Bella found in her life.

There are times in my office I take the liberty to share parts of my story, when it is appropriate. I remember one client tearing up after telling her that I too, am a partner. It meant a lot to her that I could relate. Some of the stories I hear are horrendous. The betrayal consist of much more that I experienced. However, I remember a dear friend of mine, whose husband had an affair, saying to me as I compared my loss to hers, "it doesn't matter; the betrayal hurts regardless of what it is."

Françoise

"Once again, the pain, fear, insecurity, and agony of spouses beginning the journey were so clear. I grieve with those discovering their partner's sexual addiction. I experience it with them as I experience the sheer agony on their faces and the tears in their eyes. As group leaders, we have cried with and for many of the spouses in our groups. Many times I have wished that there was a magic wand I could wave and make the pain go away. Magic wands only exist in fairy tales. Fairy tales make for great dreams. After the last 'they lived happily ever after' there is a return to the real world. The movie ends and reality returns. There is no princess that lives forever and the good guy doesn't always win." (SOSA, p. 171)

Many have told me through the years that they wish they had realized there was "help out there." It's just not the kind of help you would of imagined needing. It has forever changed you, and many things will never be the same again, including yourself. Some of have said, "I wouldn't change a thing, and others wish they had known about the help out there, it may have been different. Whatever the case, you may be saying "I never signed up for this." As hard as it was and still is in different ways, as badly as it feels and as painful as it was to be in the darkest part of it; you're here, despite that you might have wanted to give up in so many places of your life. You are here, and just "being" with yourself in the here and now is good. Relish in this moment, to honor yourself, a nice blue pleasurable zone to be. You have almost made it through your workbook. The assignments and stories are part of your story, part of your healing. Richard and I are forever grateful to have been a part of this journey with you. As therapists, we have been blessed to share in the journey with many partners of sex addicts. We have been there to walk through the highs and lows; and the gift to us, as practitioners, is the inner healing that takes place in the hearts and lives of our clients. We have seen beauty come from the rubble of pain, abandonment and betrayal. We have seen anger and depression turn into joy and hope. Partners of sex addicts share unique experiences. Their stories are sacred.

Listed below are "pearls of wisdom" from people who have been on the journey for years. They are your advisors; moms, young and older women, professionals, women who initially had no idea how life would land after discovery. Addiction has no preference to status, color or location, and these women and men were caught up in their spouse's betrayal and experienced the impact no matter who they are.

Proverbs 24:6 says, "Victory is won through many advisors."

On pages 173–174 (SOSA) there is a description of each "pearl of wisdom." As you read through the explanation of each pearl, take your time to sit with each one and jot down any thought, feeling or image that may come to mind. Don't be quick to judge yourself. The wisdom and understanding on these pages come from women who care about making a difference in your life. They are meant to be gentle reminders that "the story is not over yet." We all have places to grow, and their advice comes from a place of pain and growth in their own lives.

Take your time with each pearl, and notice how and where in your body you experience what comes up for you. If it feels like a threat response coming at you, slow it down, be curious and notice what and where you are with this. Take a moment to look around and breathe.

1. Don't blame yourself for the addict's problem.

"So do not fear, for I am with you; do not be dismayed, for I am your God. I will strengthen you and help you; I will uphold you with my righteous right hand." Isaiah 41:10 NASB

Is there anything in the past that comes up for you around this issue and you would like to do differently now?

2. Face your own trauma.

"Make me know Thy ways, O Lord. Teach me Thy paths. Lead me in Thy truth and teach me. For Thou art the God of my salvation." Psalms 25:4–5 NASB

Is there anything in the past that comes up for you around this issue and you would like to do differently now?

---

3. Don't minimize the grief and pain.

"I will lead the blind by ways they have not known, along unfamiliar paths I will guide them; I will turn the darkness into light before them and make the rough places smooth. These are the things I will do; I will not forsake them." Isaiah 42:16

4. Is there anything in the past that comes up for you around this issue and you would like to do differently now?

---

5. Face your own trauma.

"The poor and needy search for water, but there is none; their tongues are parched with thirst. But I the Lord will answer them; I, the God of Israel, will not forsake them." Isaiah 41:17

Is there anything in the past that comes up for you around this issue and you would like to do differently now?

6. Extend trust slowly.

"My shield is God Most High, who saves the upright in heart." Psalms 7:10

Is there anything in the past that comes up for you around this issue and you would like to do differently now?

7. Don't make a decision on the relationship for at least one year.

"Trust in the Lord with all your heart, and do not lean on your own understanding. In all your ways acknowledge Him, and He will make your path straight."
Proverbs 3:5, 6

Is there anything in the past that comes up for you around this issue and you would like to do differently now?

8. Acknowledge your powerlessness and surrender control over the addiction.

"Though the fig tree should not blossom, and there be no fruit on the vines. Though the yield of the olive tree shall fail. And the fields produce no fruit. Though the flock should be cut off from the fold. And there be no cattle in the stalls. Yet, I will exult in the Lord. I will rejoice in the God of my salvation. The Lord God is my strength. And He has made my feet like hinds' feet. And makes me walk on high places." Habakkuk 3:17–19 NASB

Is there anything in the past that comes up for you around this issue and you would like to do differently now?

9. Identify your coping skills.

"Heed instruction and be wise, and do not neglect it. Blessed is the man who listens to me, Watching daily at my gates, Waiting at my doorposts. For he who finds me finds life And obtains favor from the Lord." Proverbs 8:33–35 NASB

Is there anything in the past that comes up for you around this issue and you would like to do differently now?

10. Be honest about your emotions, even with God.

"Listen to my words, Lord, consider my lament. Hear my cry for help, my King and my God, for to you I pray." Psalms 5:1, 2

Is there anything in the past that comes up for you around this issue and you would like to do differently now?

11. Give up the martyr/savior complex.

"Pride brings a person low, but the lowly in spirit gain honor." Proverbs 29:23

Is there anything in the past that comes up for you around this issue and you would like to do differently now?

12. Destroy the emotional measuring tape.

"I praise you because I am fearfully and wonderfully made; your works are wonderful, I know that full well." Psalms 139:14

Is there anything in the past that comes up for you around this issue and you would like to do differently now?

| |
| |
| |
| |
| |
| |
| |

13. Retire the private eye badge.

"Listen to my cry; for I am in desperate need; rescue me from those who pursue me, for they are too strong for me. Set me free from my prison, that I may praise your name. Then the righteous will gather about me because of your goodness to me." Psalms 142:6, 7

Is there anything in the past that comes up for you around this issue and you would like to do differently now?

| |
| |
| |
| |
| |

14. Self-care is critical.

"Do you not know that your bodies are temples of the Holy Spirit, who is in you, whom you have received from God? You are not your own; [20] *you were bought at a price. Therefore honor God with your bodies."* 1 Corinthians 6:19, 20

Is there anything in the past that comes up for you around this issue and you would like to do differently now?

| |
| |
| |
| |
| |
| |
| |
| |

15. Your recovery is important.

How will you make it a priority?

| |
| |
| |
| |
| |
| |

"A final personal story and verse that was life changing for me: As I sat on the park bench feeling hopeless and despaired, my dear friend said "I see the vision for you; I have the hope for you." When I could not feel or see what she saw for me, I hung on to what she believed, and the verse that God gave me at that time was." Habakkuk 1:5; 2:3.

"Look at the nations and watch—and be utterly amazed. For I am going to do something in your days that you would not believe, even if you were told." (Habakkuk 5:1)

"For the revelation awaits an appointed time; it speaks of the end and will not prove false. Though it linger, wait for it; it will certainly come and will not delay." (Habakkuk 2:3)

The timing of this was right after graduate school. I was so excited to start my own practice and do the things that I now do, but the jobs weren't there, and after years of working hard to get to that point, it was very disappointing. I am astonished and I wonder over an awesome God, because He has never let me down. Have faith and courage, dear friend. God is doing something amazing in your life. You may not believe it now; "the revelation awaits an appointed time."

Find a place that is comfortable and experience what it feels like to have opened up and been authentic and vulnerable with yourself and others about some of the darkest hours of your life. Take a moment; reflect on this journey and what it was like for you. Give yourself credit for having the courage to do the hard work.

You may need to go back to your workbook every now and then and re-experience some of your exercises for hope and encouragement. 12-step meetings often begin with the words "through the doors of this room walked the most courageous people we know." You have faced some very difficult parts of your story and as a result, you have become a stronger healthier self. You have the capability to stay true to yourself wherever you are in your process of healing, because of who you are and whose you are. As Dr. Robert A. Cook says, and I would say to my children on their way out to school in the morning, Walk with the King.

Hope for the Heart

My challenge for today is:

Françoise's Story

Pearls of Wisdom: Learning from the Voice of Experience

In no way do I think I am the expert on the subject of sexual addiction and how it impacts the partner in all aspects of her/his life. I offer my heart from the voice of experience. If there were only two things I could share with you, it would be "His grace is sufficient for all your needs, and take the time you need to heal." Don't rush through the grieving process. You want to be able to develop strength and resilience in the aftermath of trauma.

The exposure to an extreme stressor such as sexual addiction ruptures the very core of your trust, a key element in a safe and healthy relationship. It takes time to renegotiate your system after the devastating shock that your body has been through. His grace is sufficient for all your needs. He loves to prove that to us over and over again, what an awesome God we have. He is the one who restores and replenishes what you need to heal and overcome the wounds in the battle of sexual addiction. He cares about your heart, and holds it ever so gently. He desires fellowship with you, and He knows our needs before we know them.

He made us in the likeness of His Son. God sees us as perfect, because of what Jesus did on the cross for us. He died to take away our sins. I believed this thirty-nine years ago when I accepted Christ as my Savior, and I still believe today that by confessing my sins, God granted me eternal life through the blood of Christ. It is no longer I who live, but Christ in me. I continue to sin, and I continue to confess, knowing by faith God forgives me. We are not perfect beings, but desire to be more like Him in all of our imperfections.

My deepest sorrow is when I sin against God; when I hurt the heart of the one I love the most. The times I choose to be defiant, proud, and disobedient of His ways, wanting my way and not what He wants as best for me. In those moments, I feel separated and distanced from Him, even though in my heart I know He has never left me. It is my loss. I lose the connection that I so desperately need and want from Him, and yet can so easily thrust it aside. He never leaves us, He is always there, open handed and desiring to meet us where we are.

You are enough; in Him we are enough. Because we live in a broken world, we are a broken people. If there is something that needs fixing, trust the only one that will never fail you or forsake you help you with it. He has all the time you need; He is never in a hurry. We are spiritual beings and our need for spirituality is what scientist call a "God spot" in our brain, a distinctive area in the brain that is responsible for spirituality. Feed your brain, and feed your heart with the love that only God can fill.

God might be prompting you to share your story with someone; trust Him, and by faith believe that He loves you, and has the utmost best interest at hand for you. He won't take you in places that you are not equipped for. It's one step in the water, and He is just on the other side reaching out to walk you through the storms and the calm. Take the time you need in the arms of Jesus. He will heal you and help you process the wounds, and bring people alongside to support you.

Slow yourself down. Feel what you feel. Get help from professionals who are trained in the field of sex addiction and the trauma model. Use your resources; friends and family who are supportive and not judgmental. Take time out for you. Even the slightest things can make a huge difference in our well-being. I remember how taking baths felt very cleansing for me, emotionally and physically. It slowed me down and I could cry a dozen tears as I cried out to God and felt every emotion there was to feel. God's grace was sufficient and I heard Him in the stillness of my voice; "I am here with you, I will never leave you or forsake you." He never has, and I am who I am today because of His grace.

God bless you in your journey.

Françoise

My Journal

My thoughts for today:
My feelings:
What am I sensing in my body?
Can I put any meaning to my experiences?
What can I be thankful for today?

APPENDIX

The last page is provided for your continued growth and self-care. Please make copies and maintain your journey to a better, stronger, more courageous You…

This is your story; every feeling and thought expressed in your journal is a precious part of you. You have been diligent to work hard at the ability to be present and aware of your internal experience and broader external self. Thank you for allowing me to have been a small part of this with you. For this I am forever grateful.

Françoise

My Ninety Day Journal to Positive Self-Care

Day_____:
What I notice today:
Emotionally:
Behaviorally:
Physically:
Relationally:
Personally:
Spiritually:
Thoughts, feelings, and experiences I am having today that keep me from being in the moment:
Thoughts and behaviors I will use to replace the old and put on the new: